UND[illegible]ED SCENES

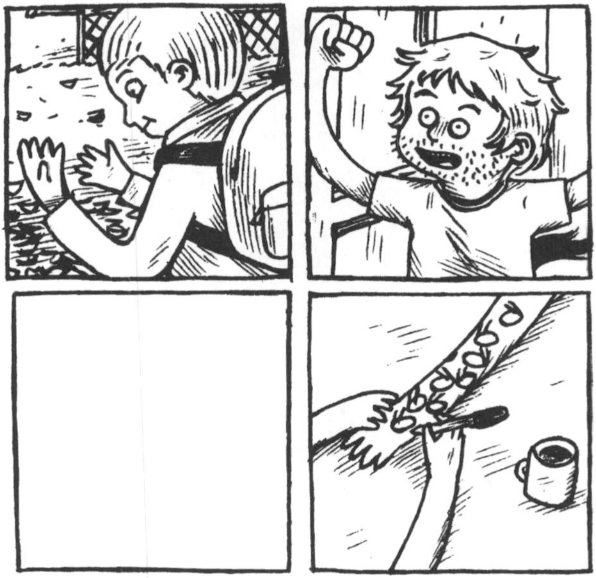

JEFFREY BROWN

PUBLISHED BY TOP SHELF PRODUCTIONS
P.O. BOX 1282
MARIETTA GA 30061-1282
USA

PUBLISHERS: BRETT WARNOCK + CHRIS STAROS
 VISIT OUR ONLINE CATALOG AT: WWW.TOPSHELFCOMIX.COM

FIRST PRINTING. MAY 2010
PRINTED IN CANADA

ISBN 978-1-60309-058-2

ALTHOUGH MUCH OF THIS BOOK IS AUTOBIOGRAPHICAL, IT SHOULD NOT BE VIEWED AS A NECESSARILY TRUE OR ACCURATE PORTRAYAL OF ANY OF THE EVENTS DIPICTED, NOR OF ANY OF THE PEOPLE WITHIN OR THEIR CHARACTER, AND IN ANY CASE IT ALSO CONTAINS A DECENT AMOUNT OF OUTRIGHT FICTION.

CONTENTS

WHY AUTOBIOGRAPHY?
PEOPLE OFTEN ASK ME WHY I WRITE AUTOBIOGRAPHY...
YEAH, WHY DO YOU WRITE ABOUT YOURSELF ALL THE TIME?
I'M NOT REALLY WRITING ABOUT ME. I MEAN, I DON'T EVEN REALLY LOOK LIKE THIS EXACTLY.
WHAT I'M REALLY TRYING TO WRITE ABOUT IS LIFE-EXPERIENCES, FEELINGS, SITUATIONS... THE THINGS WE ALL GO THROUGH.
I DON'T THINK LIFE HAS TO BE "INTERESTING" AS MUCH AS I THINK IT SHOULD BE MEANINGFUL.
FOR ME, THAT'S THE WHOLE PURPOSE OF ART - TO BETTER UNDERSTAND LIFE, AND FIND MEANING IN IT.
BY SHOWING THESE PIECES OF MY LIFE, I HOPE THAT OTHERS CAN LEARN SOMETHING NEW ABOUT THEIR OWN LIFE.

WHEN WILL MY SUPERPOWERS MANIFEST THEMSELVES?

MY BROTHER KNOWS KUNG FU

SURPRISE

snicker
HA HA!
SMACK
HEY! I'M BLEEDING
SORRY. YOU SHOULDN'T SURPRISE ME RIGHT AFTER KUNG FU CLASS
MAYBE I'LL TELL MOM AND DAD..

BIRTHDAY GIFT

WHAT THE HELL? THIS ISN'T G.I.JOE.
OH... IT'S A BOOK.
WHAT'S IT FOR?
IT'S FOR MAKING LITTLE PAPER CONSTRUCTIONS.
DOUG PICKED IT OUT HIMSELF.
FLIP
FLIP
FLIP

YOU LIKE MAKING THINGS OUT OF CARDBOARD AND STUFF... YOU DO THAT KIND OF THING...
I DO?
WHAT'S NEXT?

SQUISH
SQUISH
SQUISH
DOUGLASSS!!
HEE HEE
HEEHEE
HA HA HA

TICKLE

LET'S TICKLE JEFF
NO STOP!
HA HA HA NO HA
HEE HEE
HA!
HA HA!
BRAPPPP!
HA HA
HEE HEE
HA HA
BRAP! BRAP!
HA HA STOP!

LUNCHBOX

LOOK AT THE PUSSIES!
HAW!
WHAT'D YOU SAY?
SHOVE
HAHA
SHOVE
SMAK!
UH!
WUMP

ELBOW

HEE HEE HEE
HEE HEE
RRR
CLIK
CLIK
LET ME IN!!
HEE HA
HA HA
BAM
BANG
CRASH!
OH SHIT!
KLIK
KLAK
HOLY SHIT!
GET SOME TOWELS!

NUNCHUCKS

SPANK

YOU LITTLE BUGGER!
DOUGLAS!
I told you you'd get a spanking!
NO!
dodge
SMACK!
WHERE ARE MOM AND DAD GOING?
TO THE EMERGENCY ROOM.
I DON'T THINK DAD'S GOING TO SPANK US ANYMORE

WRASSLIN'

OKAY, OKAY, I GIVE!
YOU SHOULD WRESTLE DOUG NOW.
NO
I THOUGHT YOU'RE SUPPOSED TO BE THE GRAPPLING EXPERT. SCARED?
NO.
GIVE UP!
NO!
OKAY, I GIVE, I GIVE
YOU'RE TOO FAT
CLAP CLAP

NO HOLDS BARRED

REDWINGS

DID THEY WIN?
NO, IT'S IN OVERTIME
OOOH!
QUIET PLEASE
SORRY DAD
SCORE!
YAAAYYYY!
C'MON NOW!
WOO HOO!
YES!
WE WERENT DOING ANYTHING
THEN WHO THREW THIS SHIRT ON MY HEAD?!
HEE HEE

SNAP

WHAT ARE YOU GETTING?
UM, LEMON-HEADS, ALEXANDE THE GRAPES...
HEY STUPIDS!
FUCK YOU!
HAHA
HA HA HA
SNAP!
SNAP!
SNAP!
SNAP!
STOP!
LEAVE US ALONE!
SNAP!
SNAP!
SNAP!

WHERE'S MOM AND DAD?
WHAT'S WRONG?
THERE'S TWO GUYS ON BIKES TRYING TO FIGHT US OR SOMETHING
WHERE?
AT THE END OF THE STREET

WHY ARE YOU MESSING WITH MY FAMILY?
I WASN'T
THEN WHY DID MY BROTHER COME HOME CRYING?
DON'T EVER BOTHER MY FAMILY AGAIN
KOFF KOFF

CHIMNEY PREFERENCE
LET'S GO HOME
OKAY
WHERE'S HE GOING?

SMACK!
WHAT'RE YOU DOING?
WHAT DO YOU MEAN?
THAT'S NOT HOW YOU STOP.
BUT THAT'S THE ONLY WAY I KNOW HOW TO

FEEBLE ATTEMPTS 1987

MOST LIKELY SUPER POWER*:

SHOOTING ELECTRICTY OUT OF HANDS

(* SECOND MOST LIKELY: STEEL CLAWS GROWING OUT OF FOREARMS)

LATER...
LOOK!
THAT KID SAW US!
GET HIM!
NEVER!
AAUUGHH!
KAPOW!
WE THOUGHT WE WERE DEAD, BUT SUDDENLY THERE WAS A FLASH OF LIGHT..
IF ONLY I COULD TELL THEM IT WAS I WHO SAVED THEIR LIVES...

NO ONE MUST KNOW

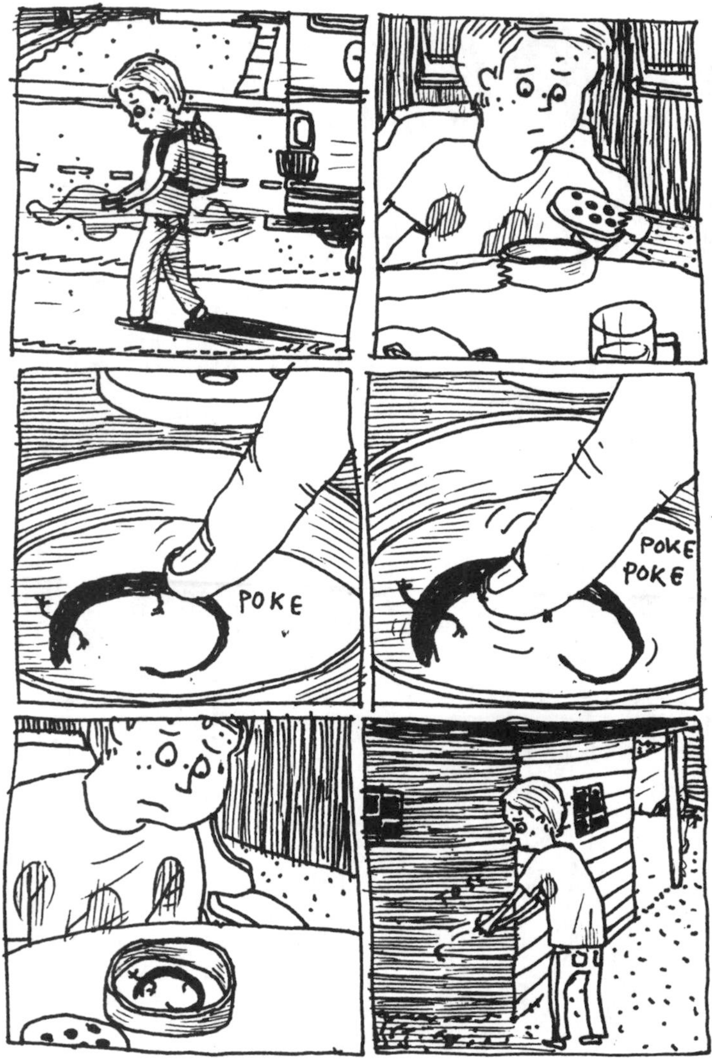
POKE
POKE
POKE

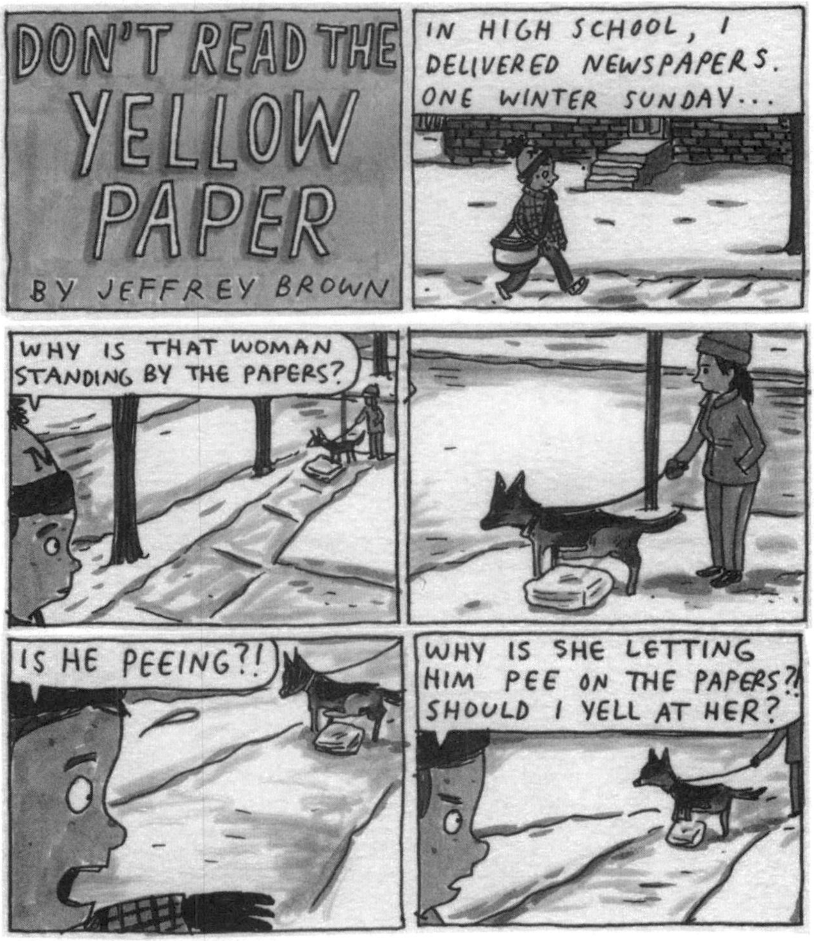
DON'T READ THE YELLOW PAPER
BY JEFFREY BROWN
IN HIGH SCHOOL, I DELIVERED NEWSPAPERS. ONE WINTER SUNDAY...
WHY IS THAT WOMAN STANDING BY THE PAPERS?
IS HE PEEING?!
WHY IS SHE LETTING HIM PEE ON THE PAPERS?! SHOULD I YELL AT HER?

MAYBE NOT...
...I'M TOO FAR AWAY FOR HER TO HEAR, BUT NOW SHE'S LEAVING...
GOOD THING THE BUNDLES ARE WRAPPED IN PLASTIC.
IS THAT REALLY PEE?!
BUT... BUT...
WHY WOULD SOMEONE HAVE THEIR DOG PEE ON THE NEWSPAPERS?!
www.topshelfcomix.com

HELP, I'M DROWNING!

SPLASH
SPLASH
SPLASH
HUH... SO THAT'S WHAT UNDERTOW FEELS LIKE
SPLASH
SPLASH
SPLASH
AH!
SPLASH
SPLASH
ACK! CAN'T-- BLEH--HELFPH!
DO YOU NEED SOME HELP JEFF?
SPLASH
ACK! COUGH! SPUTTER!
SPLASH
SPLASH
SPLASH
THANKS SEAN
SPLASH
SPLASH

DUDE, SERIOUSLY!
ARE THOSE ALL LED ZEPPELIN?
YEAH, I BORROWED THEM FROM NATE TO COPY..
HEY NICK
ARE THOSE NEW GLASSES?
YEAH, CHECK THEM OUT- THEY'RE UNBREAKABLE!
TWIST
SCRUNCH
TORQUE
SNAP!
OH.

I WAS A LEVEL 15 JERK
BY JEFFREY BROWN
WE USED TO PLAY DUNGEONS & DRAGONS ON THE BUS BACK IN HIGH SCHOOL
ME
PAUL
TIM
BEN
DAN
Dungeon Master Nate
GUYS, I'M KIND OF TIRED OF PLAYING D&D. I THINK I'M GOING TO QUIT
YOU CAN'T QUIT!
YEAH.
YOU HAVE TO WAIT UNTIL YOUR CHARACTER IS KILLED.
..OKAY
URGH
CHOK!
UM, YOU NEED TO MAKE A SAVE ON D20, PAUL

HEY! YOU CAN'T DO THAT!
YEAH! ISN'T HE LAWFUL-GOOD OR SOMETHING?
HEH
ACKKK
RETRIBUTION WAS SWIFT AND COMPLETE...
I CAST ANOTHER FIREBALL
I PICK UP JEFF'S DIS-MEMBERED ARM AND BEAT HIM WITH IT.
SOMEHOW, PAUL'S CHARACTER SURVIVED...
OHHHH
...BUT EVENTUALLY HE SUCCUMBED TO HIS WOUNDS.
WHAT'S THE ROLL?
TWO.
I'M SORRY PAUL.
PAUL AND I WATCHED AS THE QUEST ENDED WITH EVERYONE ELSE GETTING EATEN BY A DRAGON.
NO HARD FEELINGS?
FIN

UNDERNEATH
HEY, DO YOU GUYS WANT TO SEE MY TUNNEL?
YOUR TUNNEL?
I'VE BEEN WORKING ON IT ALL SUMMER..
HOLY CRAP! DO YOUR MOM AND DAD KNOW YOU DUG THIS IN THEIR BACKYARD?
NO. DO YOU WANT TO COME IN AND SEE?
UM...
ENTRANCE HIDDEN BY GRASS COVERED BOARD
REINFORCING BARRELS
TINY SPACE
NO, THAT'S OKAY...
THIS IS RAD..

BACKING UP
OH SHIT!
UM, MOM, I MISSED THE BUS. CAN YOU DRIVE ME TO SCHOOL?
WHAT?! WHY DO YOU DO THIS? GOD BLESS IT.
GO GET THE CAR OUT OF THE GARAGE WHILE I GET DRESSED!
WELL I DIDN'T PLAN ON WAKING UP LATE!
STOMP
STOMP
STOMP

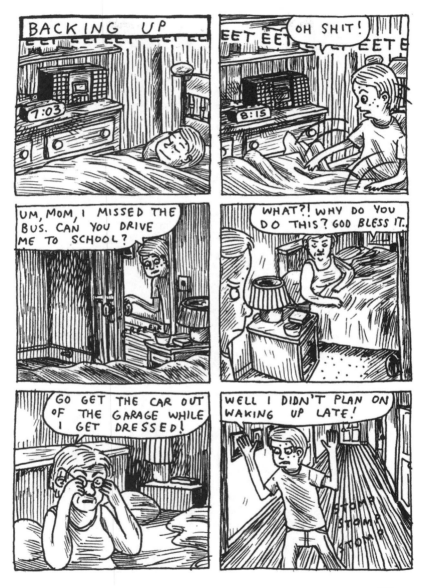

GRUMBLE GRUMBLE GRUMBLE
BRUM BRRUM
BRUM BRRUM
SSKRENNNNNCHH
OH FUCK.
UM, MOM...

CRUSTY EYES
...AND THE HORSE WAS RUNNING TOWARD THE FENCE FULL SPEED...
SO I JUMPED AND TACKLED IT WITH MY BARE HANDS AND HAD TO WRESTLE IT TO THE GROUND.
JEFF, ARE YOUR EYES OKAY?
IT'S THIS SKIN CONDITION FROM MY SCALP.
I HAVE A SPECIAL SHAMPOO TO USE THAT'LL CLEAR IT UP.
IT LOOKS LIKE IT HURTS.
I THINK I HAD IT WHEN I WAS YOUNG. MY MOM WOULD THINK I HAD GUM IN MY HAIR...
WHAT IS THIS GUNK IN YOUR HAIR?
I DON'T KNOW.
SHE'D PICK AND SCRUB, AND MY SCALP WOULD BLEED A LITTLE.
OW!
THIS WOULDN'T HAPPEN IF YOU DIDN'T CHEW GUM IN BED!
BUT I DIDN'T HAVE ANY GUM!

I HAD KILLED BEFORE, AND I WOULD KILL AGAIN.
1992
...AND SHOOT BIRDS AND STUFF..
I DON'T WANT TO SHOOT BIRDS THOUGH
HERE.
YOU CAN SHOOT A TREE
CLACK
PUMP
PUMP
PUMP
PUMP
PUMP
HEY, I CAN SEE A BIRD ON THAT TREE...
I'LL JUST HIT THE BRANCH. I WONDER IF I COULD HIT THE BIRD. I COULD HIT THE BRANCH..

SHIT! NATE! I THINK I KILLED IT.
I KILLED IT NATE. I THINK I KILLED IT.

CUTE GIRLS ARE CUTE!

I like cheese

hat

HI JEFF
HI
I LIKE THE TOP OF YOUR HAT--
HEY!
FWAP
FWAP
OW
HOW'D YOU LIKE IT IF I HIT YOUR HEAD?
I WAS TRYING TO BE NICE TO YOU, JERK
WHY DON'T YOU TRY TO GO HOME, YOU STUPID JERK

recess

WOW. THE NEW GIRL IS SO CUTE. I THINK I LIKE HER
DON'T TELL SCOTT BUT I LIKE THE NEW GIRL
I LIKE THE NEW GIRL.
DON'T TELL BRIAN THAT, THOUGH

smurf

CAN YOU DRAW A SMURF?
YEAH
HA HA! THAT'S PERFECT! THANKS
THANKS JEFF. THAT WAS SWEET OF YOU.
HUH?
THE SMURF DRAWING YOU GAVE TO CHAS TO GIVE TO ME
HE GAVE YOU THAT? I DREW THAT BECAUSE HE ASKED ME TO...

poetry is sexy

girls are stupid

HI.
HI.
HOW WAS YOUR WEEKEND?
IT WAS OKAY.
MAN, I WAS A LOSER IN HIGH SCHOOL AND NOW THAT I'M MARRIED ALL THESE CUTE YOUNGER GIRLS ALL HANG ON ME..

thanks anyway

I'M USELESS

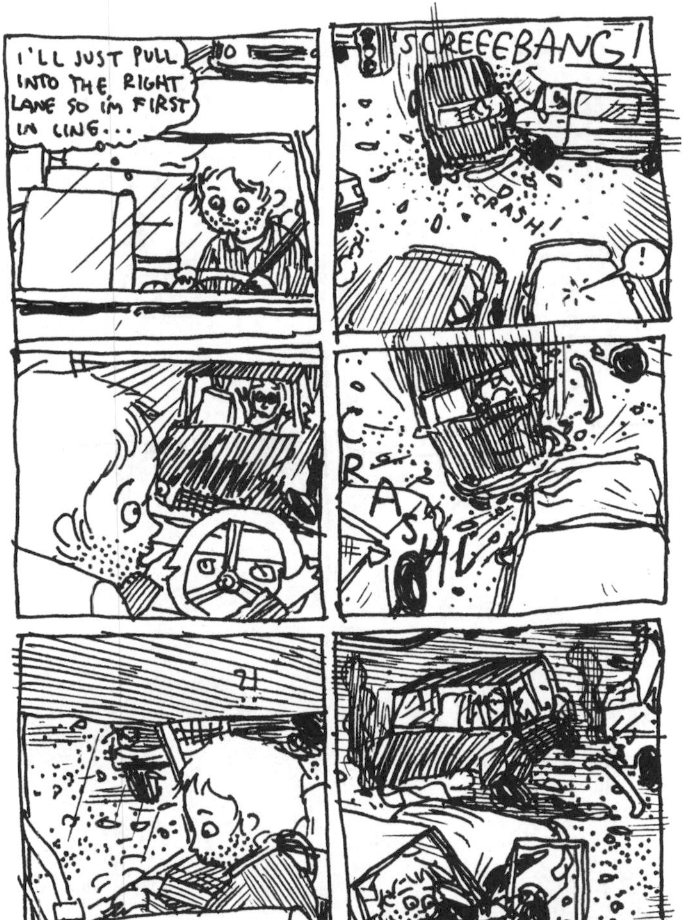
I'LL JUST PULL INTO THE RIGHT LANE SO I'M FIRST IN LINE...
SCREEEBANG!
CRASH!
!
CRASH!
?!

ARE YOU OKAY?
I DONT KNOW
UM, WHAT'S YOUR NAME?
SOB
UH... DONT WORRY HELP'S COMING, OKAY?
SOB

SNOW PARKING

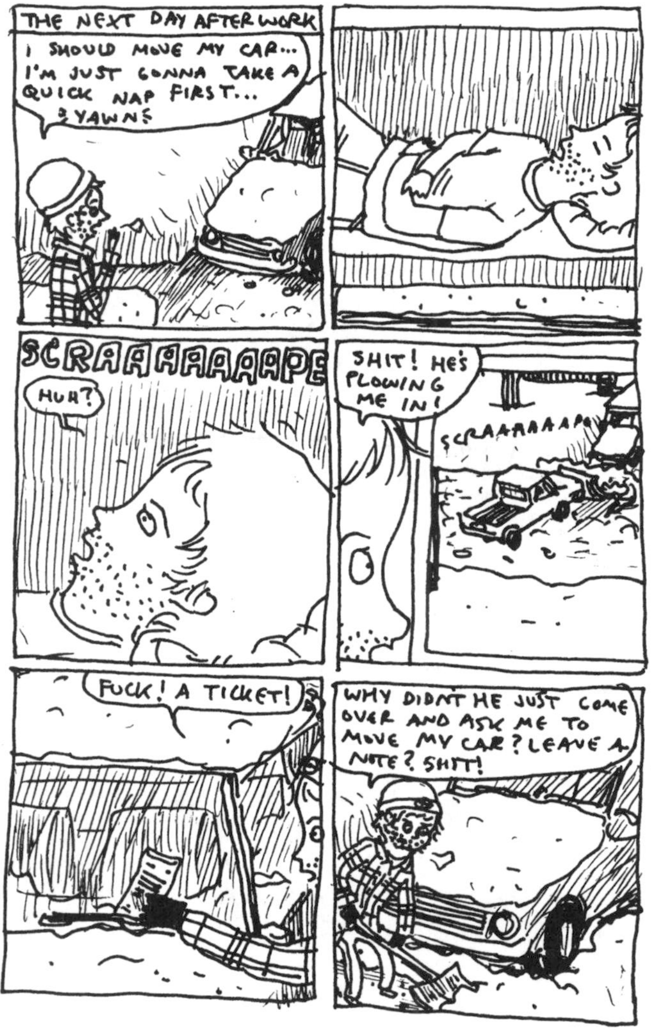
THE NEXT DAY AFTER WORK
I SHOULD MOVE MY CAR... I'M JUST GONNA TAKE A QUICK NAP FIRST... ≷YAWN≶
SCRAAAAAAAAAPE
HUH?
SHIT! HE'S PLOWING ME IN!
SCRAAAAAAAP
FUCK! A TICKET!
WHY DIDN'T HE JUST COME OVER AND ASK ME TO MOVE MY CAR? LEAVE A NOTE? SHIT!

GOOD. YOU'RE MOVING YOUR CAR... I WAS GOING TO GIVE YOU A TICKET
YOU ALREADY GAVE ME A TICKET. I'M SORRY--
YOU THE OWNER OF THE PROPERTY?
YEAH
I'VE NEVER SEEN THAT CAR IN MY LIFE
I SAID I WAS SORRY
I LIVE ACROSS THE STREET! I'M PARKED OUT THERE EVERY DAY!
JUST MOVE YOUR CAR
I AM. I HAVE TO SHOVEL IT OUT
THAT'S GOOD ENOUGH. C'MON. NOW.
@#$?★!

WHY I CAN'T EAT RAMEN NOODLES
THERE ARE MANY IMPORTANT LESSONS TO LEARN IN COLLEGE. LIKE DISCOVERING RAMEN NOODLES!
ONLY 19¢?!
Ramen NoodleSoup Chicken Flavor
THEY'RE SUPER-EASY TO MAKE!
BOIL!
STIR!
EAT!
YOU CAN EAT A WHOLE MEAL AND STILL HAVE MONEY LEFT FOR OTHER IMPORTANT PURCHASES!
VODKA! MY FAVORITE!

I'VE GOT MY FIFTH OF VODKA. LET'S PLAY...
THE DAVID LYNCH'S DUNE DRINKING GAME!
HOW TO PLAY: EVERY TIME THE WORD "SPICE" IS SPOKEN IN THE FILM, YOU HAVE TO TAKE A DRINK.
...THE SPICE MELANGE...THE SPICE EXTENDS LIFE..
COULD THE SPICE AFFECT US...
...THE SPICE EXPANDS CONSCIOUSNESS. THE SPICE...
WHERE THERE'S SPICE AND SPICE MINING..
HE WHO CONTROLS THE SPICE...
SOON
THE WORM ISH THE SPICE, THE SPICE ISH THE WORM

I'M HUNGRY
I'LL MAKE SHOME RAMEN!
THERE!
HALFWAY THROUGH THE FILM...
THE SPICE! IT'S IN EVERYTHING HERE...
SPICE... WHAT IS IT DOING TO ME?
THE SPICE!
...DESTROY ALL SPICE PRODUCTION...
THE WORM IS THE SPICE... THE SPICE IS THE WORM
...RESTORE SPICE PRODUCTION...
EMPTY
I'LL MAKE SOME MORE RAMEN...

IS THIS COOKED ENOUGH?
OOPS!
IT'S OKAY
ADD FLAVOR
MMMM
TASTES REALLY FUNNY
MAYBE I DIDN'T STIR IT ENOUGH?
OH WELL, TOO LATE NOW.

SOON ENOUGH
SHTOP SHPINNING ROOM!
OHHHHHHHHH
BLEARGH!
IT LOOKED LIKE A BIG, FRESH BOWL OF PLAIN RAMEN NOODLES...
THE NEXT DAY
DOES ANYONE WANT ALL MY RAMEN NOODLES?
STILL...
IT'S NOT YOUR FAULT, VODKA. I FORGIVE YOU.
THE END.

PAINTIN' THE TOWN
JEFFREY BROWN

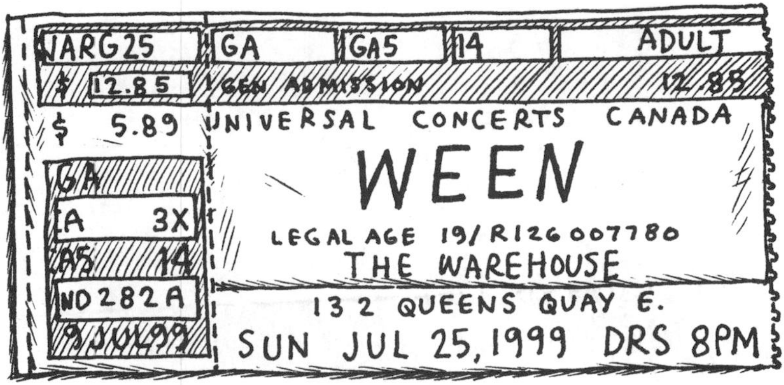

NARG25
GA
GA5
14
ADULT
$ 12.85
GEN ADMISSION
12.85
$ 5.89
UNIVERSAL CONCERTS CANADA
WEEN
GA
A 3X
A5 14
ND282A
9JUL99
LEGAL AGE 19/R126007780
THE WAREHOUSE
132 QUEENS QUAY E.
SUN JUL 25, 1999 DRS 8PM

LIVING IN GRAND RAPIDS, MICHIGAN, SEEING A ROCK SHOW USUALLY REQUIRED A ROAD TRIP
THE OIL CHANGE GUY SAID WE MIGHT NOT MAKE IT TO TORONTO AND BACK...
YOUR CAR IS FINE, LET'S GO!
LOOK, THE GIRLS IN THAT CAR ARE SENDING US MESSAGES! WRITE THEM BACK..
YOU KNOW, THEY'RE PROBABLY ON THEIR WAY TO CANADA FOR THE LOWER DRINKING AGE...
THEY CAN'T BE THAT MUCH YOUNGER THAN US..
WWNEWS
SEXUAL ENCOUNTER WITH BIGFOOT
FINALLY, RYAN SCARED THEM OFF
DO YOU LIKE NSYNC?
THE BORDER:
WHAT CONCERT ARE YOU ON YOUR WAY TO SEE?
A BAND CALLED "WEEN"
"WEED?"
"WEEN"
W-E-E-D?
W-E-E-N

YOU'RE SEEING A CONCERT, YOU DON'T KNOW WHERE YOU'RE STAYING, AND YOU'RE ALSO GOING TO THE ZOO?
RIGHT
TAKE THIS AND PULL OVER WHERE THOSE OFFICERS ARE STANDING
CRAP
WHY'D YOU TELL HIM WE WERE GOING TO THE ZOO?
BUT IT'S THE TRUTH!
YOU NEED A HAIRCUT!
OOPS
OH CRAP
BUMP!
SO WHAT KIND OF MUSIC DOES THIS BAND "WEED" PLAY?
IT'S "WEEN." UM... THEY'RE KIND OF HARD TO DESCRIBE
UM, THOSE ARE PENS... I DRAW A LOT...
?

YOUR LICENSE SAYS YOU WERE BORN IN... 1952?!
SEE MY BIRTH CERTIFICATE HAS THE RIGHT DATE.. I HAVE THE SAME NAME AS MY DAD AND THEY GOOFED WHEN THEY GAVE ME MY LICENSE..
DESPITE OUR APPARENTLY SUSPICIOUS STORIES AND STONER APPEARANCE, THEY EVENTUALLY LET US IN.
NONE OF US EVEN SMOKE WEED*
IT WAS YOUR LONG HAIR
* AT THE TIME
WE CHECKED IN TO A HOTEL DOWNTOWN AND HEADED OUT TO FIND A BAR
OXYGEN BAR
WHAT'S AN 'OXYGEN BAR'?
YOU BREATHE IN PURE OXYGEN. IT CLEANSES THE BODY OF TOXINS. HERE IS OUR PRICE LIST.
DINNER
ISN'T IT ODD THAT WE'RE THE ONLY ONES AT THIS RESTAURANT?
WHAT ABOUT THE GUYS IN SUITS BACK THERE?
LOOK, THERE'S CLAUDE, WEEN'S DRUMMER!

AFTER A COMEDY SHOW AT SECOND CITY, WE TOOK THE SUBWAY BACK TO THE HOTEL
HOW MANY MORE STOPS?
WHY'S IT TAKING SO LONG?
OH WAIT, WE'VE BEEN GOING THE WRONG WAY. I HAD THIS MAP UPSIDE-DOWN.
AND I WAS THE SOBER ONE
"ASK A ZOOKEEPER" DAY
WHY AREN'T THE GIRAFFES ORANGE?
I THINK THAT'S JUST IN CARTOONS WHERE THEY'RE ORANGE.
NO, I'VE SEEN THEM. THEY'RE ORANGE.
WELL, MAYBE THERE'S A SUBSPECIES THAT'S JUST A LITTLE MORE ORANGISH BROWN.
ROLL
YEAH, SUBSPECIES. THAT'S WHAT I WAS GETTING AT.
SUBSPECIES.
SNICKER
HA

FINALLY, IT WAS TIME TO SEE WEEN!
LOOK, THE LINE ISN'T TOO LONG
WE GOT HERE JUST IN TIME
AS ALWAYS, WEEN PUT ON A GREAT LIVE SHOW
WITH THEIR USUAL MIX OF TECHNICAL VIRTUOSITY, HUMOR, AND BOUNDLESS ENERGY
WE'RE WEEN
MISTER WOULD YOU PLEASE
THIS GUY KEEPS BACKING INTO ME...
FINE, ACCEPTING ONLY FRE
HE'S PRETTY STONED... I'LL MOVE OVER..

CALL YOUR NAME FROM A DI
I CAN'T ESCAPE HIM
FINALLY, AFTER ALMOST THREE HOURS THE SHOW ENDS...
WHAT TIME IS IT?
TWELVE THIRTY
WE HAD DECIDED TO DRIVE HOME RIGHT FROM THE CONCERT
ARE YOU ALL U.S. CITIZENS?
YEAH
GO ON AHEAD
SOON
SOMEONE ELSE NEEDS TO DRIVE, MY EYES ARE BUGGING OUT
WE GOT HOME AT SUNRISE
I'M GLAD I DONT WORK TODAY
ME TOO

OKAY, BYE (SEPTEMBER 11 2001)

WELL, I SHOULD PROBABLY GET GOING...
OKAY,.. I JUST THOUGHT YOU'D WANT TO KNOW...
SHIT.
...ARE BEING EVACUATED AS A PRECAUTION IN DOWNTOWN CHICAGO...

ATTENTION CUSTOMERS, WE WILL BE CLOSING IN A HALF HOUR DUE TO THE TRAGEDIES IN NEW YORK AND WASHINGTON...
NPR WAS SAYING ANOTHER PLANE WENT DOWN IN PENNSYLVANIA...
I HEARD IT WAS HEADED HERE...
ARE YOU GUYS CLOSED?
YEAH, I GUESS ALOT OF PLACES ARE CLOSING...
...NO, I THINK YOU MEAN THE NORTH TOWER, NOT THE SOUTH TOWER?...OH MY...
INTERNET ACCESS $9/hr .15/MINUTE $1.00 MINIMUM
TAK TAK TAK
WE DONT SEEM TO UNDERSTAND EACH OTHER SINCE. I THINK IT'D BE BEST IF WE DIDNT TALK FOR AWHILE...
TAK TAK TAK TAK TAK TAK

ARE BEING DIVERTED TO CANADA. F-16'S ARE...
...WERE RUNNING PAST US UP THE STAIRS, RIGHT..
YOU CAME HOME EARLY TOO, HUH?
YEAH. I EVEN STOPPED AT THE COFFEE HOUSE..
MIKE'S OVER AT MATT'S, AND THEY'LL BE COMING HOME FOR DINNER LATER.

...HAS BEEN WALKING FOR HOURS, LOOKING FOR...
...JUMPING FROM THE 80TH FLOOR AND HIGHER...
YOU GUYS WATCHING THE NEWS?
OF COURSE.
SO JEFF, YOU STILL HAVE TO SHOW ME YOUR PAINTINGS...
OKAY.
THAT WAS GOOD...
YEAH, GOOD MEAL, GUYS.
THESE ARE GREAT, JEFF.
RING
RING
RING

WHAT THE? SHE'S THE ONLY ONE WITH THIS NUMBER. DIDN'T SHE GET MY EMAIL? WHY'S SHE CALLING?
RING RING
HI.
HI. DID YOU GET BLOWED UP?
NO. DID YOU?
NO. WHAT ARE YOU DOING?
MIKE'S BROTHER IS HERE. I'M SHOWING HIM MY PAINTINGS. DID YOU GET MY EMAIL?
NO. YOU SENT AN EMAIL?
YEAH.
OH. WELL, I JUST WANTED TO MAKE SURE YOU DIDN'T GET BLOWN UP.
I SHOULD LET YOU GO THEN?
YEAH, PROBABLY.
OKAY, BYE.
BYE.

BYE MATT
BYE
BYE GUYS
BYE
BYE
BYE
BYE
...YOU CAN SEE HOW THE FLIGHT PATH CHANGES DRAMATICALLY HERE...
...THESE ROCKET ATTACKS IN AFGHANISTAN ARE APPARENTLY NOT...
...MAY HAVE BEEN HEADED FOR THE WHITE HOUSE ORIGINALLY...
...TEN THOUSAND...
I THINK IT'S TIME FOR ME TO GO TO BED...
ME TOO. I WONDER IF I HAVE CLASS TOMORROW...

G'NIGHT
G'NIGHT
'NIGHT
CLICK

SORRY GRAMMY

GIRLFRIEND NO. 3

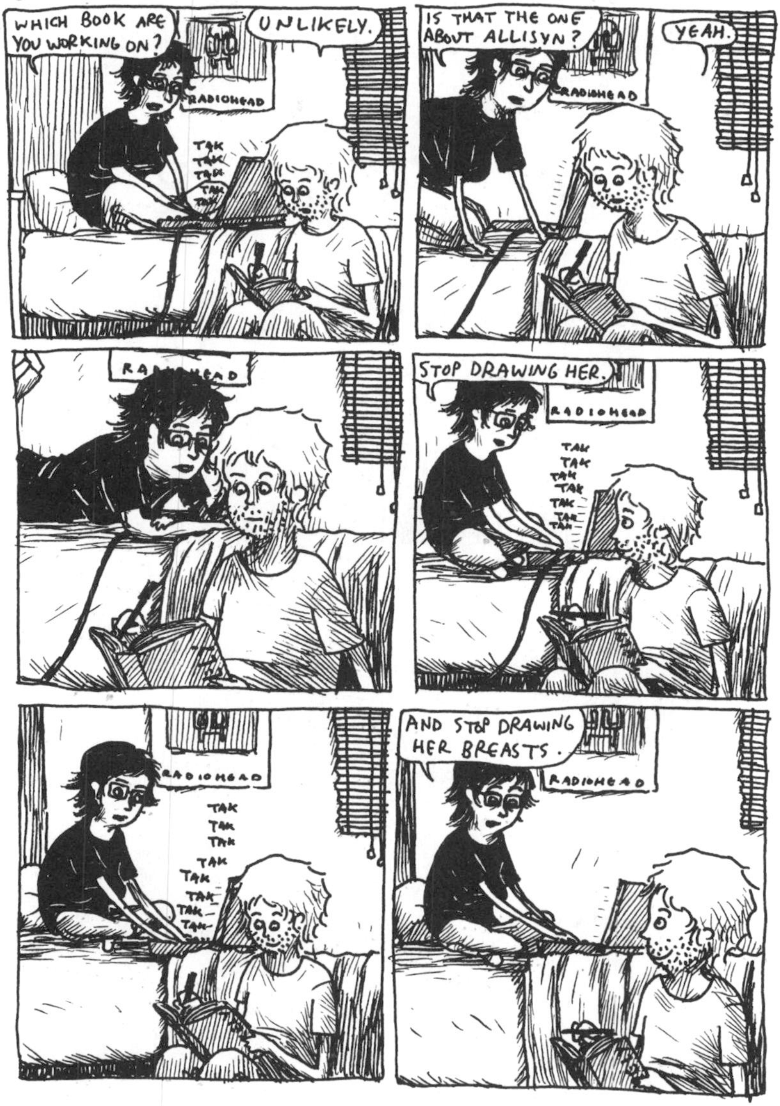

DON'T LOOK
THEM IN
THE EYE

can you feel Jesus in your heart
OH THANK YOU SIR.
can you feel Jesus
OH, GOD BLESS YOU SIR, HAVE A GOOD DAY!
Can you Feel Jesus your

OH, GOD, PLEASE HELP!
OH GOD! PLEASE, SOMEBODY HELP ME! OH JESUS!
OH GOD, SOMEBODY HELP! PLEEEEEEASE!
SIGH!
MUMBLERRRM
UHHHHH
THANK YOUUU!
ENHHH

HEY, WOULD YOU MIND SHARING A TABLE?
NOT AT ALL.
IT'S KIND OF HARD TO EXPLAIN.
YOU KNOW, TESTICULAR PLACEMENT.
WHAT?
I DON'T THINK MOST PEOPLE REALLY UNDERSTAND IT.

I'M SORRY, I JUST DON'T UNDERSTAND WHAT YOU'RE SAYING...
I WAS JUST SAYING HOW BEAUTIFUL YOUR BOOK WAS.
OH... THANK YOU..
I HAVE A BOOK TOO. HERE.
UM, WOW... UH, THIS IS REALLY... GOOD... ER..
?
YEAH.

OH, YOU, DRAWIN' THAT? THAT'S GREAT MAN, OH WOW
YEAH.
HEY, YOU KNOW WHAT? YOU SHOULD DRAW ME.
YEAH, I DRAW SOMETIMES. I'M A SCHOOLTEACHER.
HERE, I'LL SHOW YOU MY I.D. SEE?
Y'KNOW, I LIVE RIGHT AROUND HERE.
YOU SHOULD DRAW ME SOMETIME.

EEE!
HEYYY!
FUCK YOU!

DO YOU WANT TO STOP AT RECKLESS?
ACTUALLY, YEAH, I WANTED TO CHECK OUT THIS NEW BRIANWILSON
BRIAN WILSON? SERIOUSLY?
WHAT? LIKE PET SOUNDS ISN'T A WORK OF GENIUS?
YEAH, BUT C'MON.. THIS NEW LIVE ALBUM?
IT'S WORTH AT LEAST CHECKING OUT.
I TOLD YOU IT WOULDN'T BE VERY GOOD...
DUDE, YOU'RE UNBEARABLE
SORRY.
WELL, WHO'S SOMEONE YOU THINK IS JUST A GENIUS SONGWRITER?

UM, I DUNNO. DOUG MARTSCH?
WELL... ER, DOUG MARTSCH COULDN'T SONGWRITE HIS WAY OUT OF A PAPERBAG!
OOH, GOOD ONE. LOOKS LIKE YOU'LL BE THE QUICK, WITTY GUY IN THE COMEDY TROUPE...
YOU'RE EVIL.
SORRY.
YEAH. WELL, IT WAS HARD, 'CAUSE I ACTUALLY REALLY LIKE DOUG MARTSCH'S STUFF.

HEY, BUDDY, CAN YOU SPARE SOME CHANGE FOR THIS LITTLE FELLA?
WHAT'S HIS NAME?
OH YEAH, WOODSTOCK
HEY THANKS ANYWAY, YOU GUYS HAVE A GOOD NIGHT.

BIG GUY!
HEY, BIG GUY, WAIT UP! HEY, WE'RE WALKIN' THE SAME WAY, WE CAN TALK, RIGHT?
SURE.
MAN, IT'S HOT OUT, 'AINT IT?
YEP.
HEY, CAN I ASK YOU A QUESTION?
SURE.
HEY, MY CAR JUST BROKE DOWN, AND I JUST NEED A COUPLE BUCKS FOR GAS...
SORRY, MAN. I'M ALL OUT.
HEY, THANKS ANYWAY, BIG GUY.

ATTENTION---ATTENTION--
IF YOU ARE APPROACHED BY ANYONE ASKING FOR MONEY, DO NOT GIVE THEM ANY! THEY PROBABLY HAVE MORE THAN YOU DO.
METRA 6:33
METRA 7:40
-HEY-
DROP THE BAG.
WHAT? AW, MAN!
C'MON
MAN, WHY YOU ALWAYS PICKIN' ON ME? WHY DON'T YOU EVER ARREST SOMEONE LIKE HIM?
HOW DO YOU KNOW WHO WE ARREST?
OOH! NEWSPAPER.

HEY!
EXCUSE ME, DO YOU KNOW WHERE HALSTED STREET IS?
JUST A FEW BLOCKS THAT WAY.
ARE YOU HEADED THAT WAY? SAY, COULD YOU GIVE ME A RIDE? WE'RE RIGHT BY A POLICE STATION, SO YOU KNOW I'M NOT GOING TO TRY ANYTHING, RIGHT?
UM...
...OKAY...
OH, THANKS.
YEAH, I DONT HAVE A GUN OR ANYTHING! HAHA! NOT ALL OF US ARE BAD..
YOU'RE ALL RIGHT, MAN..

YEAH, I'M JUST TRYING TO GET HOME. THERE'S THIS PLACE ON HALSTED I'M SUPPOSED TO GO TO...
HERE IT IS...
WHICH WAY IS WASHINGTON?
A FEW BLOCKS NORTH.
OKAY... HEY, I REALLY APPRECIATE THE RIDE...
NO PROBLEM.
HEY, I DON'T MEAN TO BOTHER YOU, BUT... I JUST NEED A FEW DOLLARS FOR MY TICKET, AND...
SORRY... YEAH, I'M JUST TRYING TO GET TO WORK AND MAKE SOME MONEY MYSELF, Y'KNOW?
OH... YEAH... WELL, HEY, THANKS, MAN, GOD BLESS..

SAY, DO YOU TWO KNOW ABOUT THE LORD?
UM...
Y'SEE, I WAS SENT HERE TO TELL YOU ABOUT THE LORD... IT SAYS RIGHT HERE. THAT I WAS SENT... UM... IT SAYS...
WELL, I. CAN'T FIND THAT PAGE, I GUESS I DON'T HAVE IT WITH ME... BUT HERE, LOOK AT THIS...
SEE, IT SAYS THERE, THAT IF YOU BELIEVE IN JESUS YOU'LL BE SAVED... AND, UH...
MM-HM.
HERE, YOU CAN HAVE THIS... AND IT SAYS HERE... UH...
OH, IS YOUR TRAIN HERE? WELL, YOU CAN KEEP THOSE NOW... GOD BLESS YOU...
OUR TRAIN'S HERE..

HEY, DO YOU TWO NEED SOME HELP?
C'MON
HEY!
SOPHIA!
WHAT?
WE DON'T NEED HELP. WE ALREADY KNOW WHERE WE'RE GOING.
YEAH, BUT, WELL, HE WAS YELLING TO US...
HE JUST WANTED TO HELP US SO WE'D GIVE HIM SOME MONEY.
I KNOW...
YOU'RE TOO NICE SOMETIMES...

JEFF, I DONT THINK I WANT TO TONIGHT..
WHY NOT?
BECAUSE I'M ON MY PERIOD.
BUT PERIOD SEX IS JUST LIKE NORMAL SEX.
JUST A LITTLE MESSIER..
OKAY, OKAY...

MORNING.
MORNING.
YAWN
DO YOU WANT TO TAKE A SHOWER TOGETHER?
NOT REALLY.
AWW, POOR BABY.
IF WE LIVED TOGETHER, DO YOU THINK I'D STILL TRY TO GET YOU TO SHOWER WITH ME EVERY DAY?
OR WOULD I JUST TRY TWO OR THREE TIMES A WEEK?
WELL, I'D HOPE YOU TRY EVERYDAY... ACTUALLY, YEAH, I THINK YOU WOULD STILL TRY EVERY DAY..
YEAH, YOU'RE RIGHT... I WOULD TRY EVERY DAY...
YEAH..

CRY ON COMMAND
WAAHHHH!
WAAHHHHH!
THERE, THERE...
WAAHHHHH!
WAAHHHHH!
IT'S ALRIGHT...

OKAY, SON..
SAY, 'GIVE ME SOME MONEY RIGHT NOW!'
'GIVE ME SOME MONEY RIGHT NOW!'
HEYYYY, ALRIGHT!
THAT'S MY BOY!
GIVE ME SOME MONEY RIGHT NOW!
HAHAHA!

DO YOU WANTA GO PLAY SMASH BROTHERS?
YEAH...I'M ALL DRAWED OUT...
HOLY SHIT...

TAKKA TUMP
TAKKA TUMP TUMP RAPPA
TAKKA TUMP RAPPA
TAKKA TUMP RAPPA
TAKKA TUMP RAPPA
TAKKA TUMP RAPPA
TAKKA TUMP RAPPA TUMP
HEYYY, MR. BROWN... HOW ARE YOU?
MORNING MIKE
CROWN BOOKS
JINGLE JINGLE
CROWN BOOKS
CAN WE LOOK AT THE POKEMON CARDS?
SURE.
I WANT THESE FOUR PACKS...

AWWWW!
SWEET!
LEMMEE SEE!
HOW MUCH WOULD IT BE FOR THREE MORE PACKS?
JUST UNDER ELEVEN DOLLARS.
HOLD ON.
BEEP
CROWN BOOKS
HERE...
THANK YOU

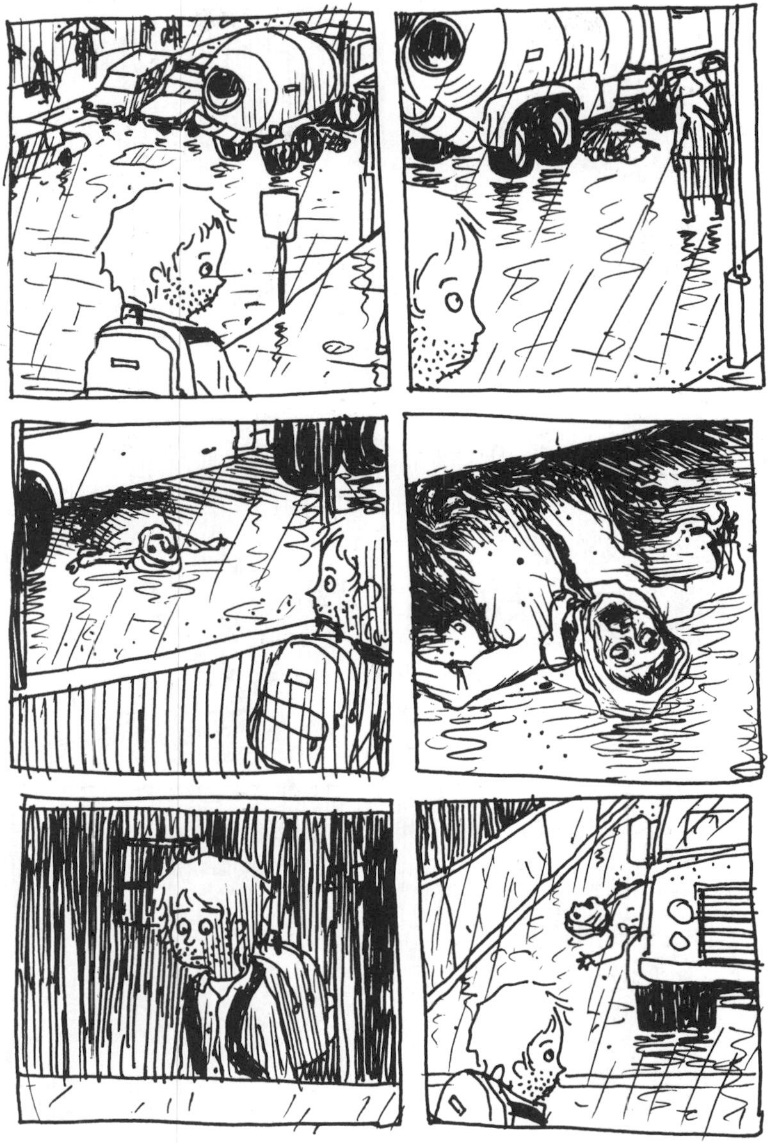

SKRITCH SKRITCH
CLICK

I'M LOOKING FOR THE BEETHOVEN STRING QUARTETS BY THE GUARENI STRING QUARTET...
OKAY... LET'S SEE HERE...
TAK TAK TAK
WELL... WE'VE GOT SOME... UM, I DONT SEE...
TAK TAK TAK TAK
AIMEE MANN
UM...
AIMEE MANN
WOULD YOU LIKE ME TO COME BACK THERE AND USE THE COMPUTER MYSELF, SINCE YOU SEEM TO BE FAIRLY INCOMPETENT?

MUSIC, CALL ON LINE FOUR
MAYBE IT'S SOPHIA..
MUSIC, THIS IS JEFF
OH. YEAH, WE HAVE PLENTY OF COPIES. IT'S ON SALE FOR 15.99. UH-HUH.
OKAY. YOU'RE WELCOME. HAVE A GOOD DAY.
NOW PLAYING
MUSIC, CALL ON LINE TWO
MAYBE IT'S SOPHIA!
FIN

JUST DON'T STOP

JEFFREY

SOPHIA

A MEDIOCRE ROMANCE

HI
HI
...AND I MADE YOU SOME COOKIES. THEY JUST GOT DONE
DO YOU WANT TO SEE MY BEDROOM?
YEAH
YAP
YAP
...AND THAT'S MY WALK IN CLOSET... AND YOU CAN SEE HOW I STARTED TO PAINT THE WALLS... AND...
SHORTLY
MPH
SO MY DAD AND BROTHER WON'T BE HOME FOR A FEW HOURS STILL...

DANG IT!
WELL HI, JEFF. SOPHIA.
HI
HI DAD.
WE'RE GLAD TO HAVE YOU. IT'S NICE WHEN FRIENDS VISIT
YEAH - THANKS FOR HAVING ME
IT'S NO PROBLEM. IT'S ALMOST LIKE A REVOLVING DOOR AROUND HERE..
DAD! IT IS NOT. IT'S BEEN A COUPLE YEARS SINCE ANYONE'S CAME..
DO WE HAVE TIME TO GET THE SPARKLERS BEFORE THE MOVIE?
YEAH
TELL ME AGAIN WHAT YOU'RE GOING TO NEED ALL THOSE SPARKLERS FOR?
IF YOU SET 600 OFF TOGETHER, IT'S REALLY COOL, IT'S LIKE, FWOOOSH!

SOPHIA? HOW ARE YOU? WHAT HAVE YOU BEEN UP TO BLAH BLAH BLAH BLAH SO GOOD TO SEE YOU AGAIN
OH HI! GOOD ARE YOU LIVING HERE BLAH BLAH BLAH BLAH BLAH BLAH BLAH BLAD SAME HERE BYE
THAT'S SO WEIRD.. THAT WAS THIS GIRL I WENT TO HIGH SCHOOL WITH.. SHE WAS THE TOTAL PARTY GIRL AND NOW SHE'S KIND OF GOODY TWO SHOES
HA!
OKAY, STAND BACK...
WOOOOOOOSHH!
THAT'S IT?
THAT WAS PRETTY COOL
IT DIDNT LAST VERY LONG...
SORRY YOU HAVE TO SLEEP ON THE COUCH..
IT'S OKAY. YOU COULD SLEEP HERE WITH ME..
HA!

WHAT TIME DO WE HAVE TO PICK YOU UP FROM DRIVER'S ED?
YAWN
ELEVEN FIFTEEN
HAVE FUN
ALL THESE FIELDS REMIND ME OF MY GRANDPARENTS' FARM..
IT'S SO BORING AND DESOLATE. SEE WHY I CAN'T LIVE HERE? I'M GOING CRAZY
YOU ARE ADDICTED TO SOAPS! WE SHOULD TAKE A SHOWER SOON, OR WE'RE GONNA BE LATE
WE SHOULD TAKE A SHOWER?
FINE. I'LL TAKE MINE FIRST
HEY! I THOUGHT YOU WEREN'T GOING TO SHOWER WITH ME?
I CHANGED MY MIND.
WE'RE ALMOST LATE PICKING UP YOUR BROTHER..
WE BETTER HURRY
SHUFFLE
SHUFFLE

MM
UMM
MPH
FOUR MINUTES LATER...
THAT WAS QUICK, JEFFREY
I DIDN'T KNOW I COULD DO IT THAT FAST
SORRY WE'RE LATE. WE'RE GOING TO TAKE YOU TO LUNCH THOUGH
OKAY
I HAVEN'T SEEN YOU THIS AFFECTIONATE SINCE DONNIE

MAKING BABIES

WHIRRRRRRRRRR
SLAP
SLAP
SLAP
KNOCK
KNOCK
KNOCK
SOPHIA?
YEAH?
TELEPHONE
UM, TELL THEM TO HOLD ON
OKAY
FLUSSHHHH
SHIT!
GIGGLE
IT WAS JUST A STUPID TELEMARKETER
DAMN TELEMARKETERS!
I TOLD MY BROTHER I WAS 'TAKING CARE OF BUSINESS'
HEE HEE

HERE, TRY THIS
IT'S GOOD
RINGGG
RINGGG
RING
HELLO? OH. WE'RE ABOUT TO LEAVE. A POTLUCK. I CAN CALL YOU TOMORR
WHO WAS THAT?
JOE
WHY'S HE CALLING?
HE WANTS TO SEE ME
SO? ARE YOU GOING TO?
WELL HE LIVES ACROSS THE STREET, IT'D BE WEIRD TO NOT SEE HIM WHILE HE'S IN TOWN.
I DON'T UNDERSTAND WHY YOU EVEN NEED TO TALK TO HIM
I DONT UNDERSTAND WHY YOU'RE BOTHERED
IT'S NOT LIKE I'M GOING TO GET BACK TOGETHER WITH HIM.
BECAUSE HE WAS SUCH AN ASSHOLE TO YOU. BECAUSE THERE'S NO REASON, SINCE HE WASN'T A GOOD FRIEND AFTERWARD EITHER.
HI SOPHIA. TOM. GLAD YOU CAME

THERE'S ME
AFTERWARD
SEE? THERE'S THE JET SKI I WANT TO BUY...
DAD, CAN YOU JUST DRIVE US HOME?
HOW ABOUT THIS?
ANNIE HALL? OKAY. I HAVENT SEEN IT..
ME EITHER
HA HA
HEE
WHAT'RE YOU DOING?
TUCKING YOU IN
SLEEP TIGHT
G'NIGHT

UGH... IT'S ROCK HARD! I DON'T KNOW WHAT I DID WRONG..
YOU CAN STILL KIND OF CHEW ON IT...
I CAN'T BELIEVE WE STAYED UP SO LATE AND IT DIDN'T TURN OUT RIGHT...
WE TRIED
MMM... I WISH YOU COULD SLEEP HERE... I WISH MY DAD WASN'T HERE...
ME TOO
MMM
BEFORE LONG...
UM, DON'T HATE ME, BUT I DON'T THINK I WANT TO HAVE SEX ANY MORE NOW...
OH..

WILL YOU STILL... YOU KNOW?
UM, YEAH
...DO YOU WANT TO GO HAVE SEX IN MY CLOSET?
SHUT
AH
EMH
UM
ANH
NG!
EHF
YOU'VE GOT TO-
MM
AH

MIGHTY SYSTEMS OF DISPLEASURE

SO YOU'RE MOVING TO MINNESOTA WITH JANET?
YEAH.
WHEN DID YOU DECIDE THIS? WERE YOU PLANNING ON TELLING ME?
I FOUND OUT A COUPLE WEEKS AGO. I WAS GOING TO TELL YOU EVENTUALLY BUT I KNEW YOU'D BE ALL UPSET.
AND YOU DIDN'T THINK I'D BE MORE UPSET THAT YOU HID IT FROM ME?
...
I MEAN, DIDNT YOU THINK IT'D BE MORE BOTHERING TO ME THAT IT'S LIKE A SECRET YOU DIDNT WANT ME TO FIND OUT ABOUT?

DO YOU THINK I'M MOVING BECAUSE OF HIM? I DON'T EVEN TALK TO HIM ANY MORE. HE HAS A NEW GIRLFRIEND. HE'S JUST A STUPID BOY.
WELL, YEAH, PARTLY IT'S HIM THAT BOTHERS ME. AND THAT IT'S OUT OF NOWHERE.
BECAUSE JANET CALLED. SHE WAS MOVING DOWN SOUTH, CHANGED HER MIND, AND ASKED ME.
SEEMS SO WISHY-WASHY. YOU COMPLAIN FOR MONTHS HOW SHE NEVER CALLS AND OUT OF THE BLUE SHE JUST ASKS YOU TO MOVE TO MINNEAPOLIS AND YOU JUST SAY YES?
JEFF, SHE'S MY BEST FRIEND. I HAVE A CONNECTION WITH HER I'VE NEVER FOUND WITH ANYONE ELSE EXCEPT MAYBE NORRIS*.
* HER HIGHSCHOOL BOYFRIEND
I DON'T UNDERSTAND WHY YOU NEVER TELL ME ANYTHING AND I'M ALWAYS THE LAST TO FIND OUT WHAT'S GOING ON WITH YOU.
ERG. BECAUSE.

ARE WE DONE HERE OR WHAT?
I GUESS.
LOOK.
ME

ARE YOU SURE?
YEAH.
CAUSE YOUR FEET REALLY NEED IT.
I KNOW
SIT DOWN.
ON THE TOILET?
NO, HERE.
OH.
ROLL YOUR PANTS UP.

NOW ME
I THINK IT'S DRY
OKAY, THIS IS THE LAST PART.
SPLASH
SPLASH
SEE? DOESN'T IT FEEL SO MUCH BETTER?
YEAH.

LITTLE EVENTS
2002
MONDAY OCTOBER 21
My Mom and Dad visit and take me to dinner.
TUESDAY OCTOBER 22
Arrive at work and there's a message that my Mom called and I get a knot in my stomach
10 AM
Dad had chest pains and he had to go to the hospital and they're doing tests right now...
Jeff, Dad stopped breathing for a minute... they revived him and now they have to do more tests... we'll call you as soon as we know anything...
2 PM
Meet John Hughes, who directed 80's movies like Ferris Bueller and Weird Science and Breakfast Club...
Are you John Hughes?
Yes.
I like your movies...
4 PM
How's your Dad?
I don't know. I'm still waiting for my Mom to call back..
8PM

Hi Jeff - Have you been trying to call?
yes
Oh. well Dad's Fine. They put Stents in and thats...
Stents? Mom, I don't even know what's wrong with Dad. Why didn't you call earlier?
1015 PM
WEDNESDAY OCTOBER 23
waiting for Amtrak to Minneapolis to visit C.
EMPIRE BUILDER WILL BE 40 MINUTES LATE
crap.
2 PM
An hour or so into the train ride I don't feel so good.
5 PM
FINALLY arrive in St. Paul
KISS KISS KISS KISS KISS KISS KISS KISS
i threw up on the train
what? why didn't you tell me?
then you wouldn't want to kiss me
11:40 PM
THURSDAY OCTOBER 24
S. has to work. I call my Dad from a coffee shop.
You're home already?
11 AM
I'm doing fine..
Meet Dave Eggers at the McSweeney's event.
It's nice to meet you.
11PM

FRIDAY OCTOBER 25
Eating at S.'s Restaurant.
Do you want some coffee too?
They caught the sniper.
Senator Wellstone is killed in a plane crash.
I was going to vote for him...
who?
S. takes me to downtown Minneapolis
I'll take you to the big Target.
um... okay..
SATURDAY OCTOBER 26
over a hundred people die in the Russian theatre siege
...I don't really like this French toast...
S. ends up working late and afterwards we get into an argument
Are you upset here? what's the business?
we take an hour walk around a lake and everything is nice again
That's the house I want.

we go see "Spirited Away" in the theatre
SUNDAY OCTOBER 27
S. drives me to the train station
I'll miss you.
we'll see each other soon.
Call me when you get home.
8 AM
Arrive at union station and miss my Metra train by a minute
Dang it! Now I'm stuck here for 2 hours...
430 PM
S. Calls and all is not well
Are you happy with our relationship?
what?
11 PM
well... I mean, I guess, maybe I just need to... let go of you...
Can we still... Can I still write you?
12 PM
MONDAY OCTOBER 28
Jonathan from This American Life calls
So we need to meet this week because the show we want to put you on would be in 3 weeks..
OKAY.

My best friend Daniel calls on his way back to Michigan from Washington state. I've seen him once in the past year.
I can catch a bus tomorrow... can I stay a few days?
Of course.
TUESDAY OCTOBER 29
I finally hear back on some comics I've sent out
Neither strip you sent me is really what I'm looking for...
Oh.
At work, me and Paul stop a guy trying to steal a DVD
He was trying to steal 'Airplane'
"Oooh, 'Airplane', I just HAVE to have it today!"
Daniel arrives
what are those?
I bought spurs while I was in Montana...
Red Wings win 3-2.
Blah Blah blah S. Blah blah Blah S. Blah blah blah S. Blah S. blah blah blah S...
S. doesn't call and I go to sleep.

SIGH
GOOD MORNING SUNSHINE
UH, BLUBOGJG HI, ULP
A
B
VENTI ICED AMERICANO WITH SKIM AND VANILLA =
$1.28
VENTI HOT CHOCOLATE =
$1.44
I NEED A VENTI ICED COFFEE
NEED, NEED, NEED. IT'S ALWAYS 'I NEED' WITH YOU, JEFF. DO YOU REALLY NEED IT?
YES.
HERE YOU GO
OOF!
JEFFREY BROWN YOU HAVE A CRUSH ON ME
HEH
HERE'S A NEW LID
HUH?
THAT ONE'S CRACKED
OH
THANKS
STOP STARING AT ME
YOU'RE STARING AT ME
FLIRT FLIRT FLIRT FLIRT
NO, I JUST MAKE EYE CONTACT WITH PEOPLE I THINK ARE NICE AND FRIENDLY
ARE YOU SAYING YOU THINK I'M NICE?
FLIRT FLIRT FLIRT FLIRT-FLIRT FLIRT FLIRT FLIRT FLIRT
I NEVER LIKED YOU.
I NEVER LIKED YOU EITHER

I'M NOT YOUR GIRLFRIEND, JEFFREY

AUGUST - OCTOBER 2003

MY TROUBLES BEGIN AUGUST 3

THE FIRST TIME I MET HER IN PERSON WE HAD COFFEE WITH A MUTUAL FRIEND AND THEY WENT TO CATCH TRAINS AND I WALKED TO MY CAR
I WAS FIDDLING WITH THE WINDOW DEFROSTER AND THINKING SHE WAS REALLY INTERESTING
CRUNCH!
IT'S MORE ROMANTIC TO THINK I WAS DISTRACTED BY MEETING HER THAN I JUST WASN'T PAYING ATTENTION

LAST NIGHT LASTED ALL MORNING

AUGUST 28

WE HELD HANDS AND TALKED AND I DREW OUR HANDS.
THEN OUR FRIEND SHOWED UP SO WE PUT OUR HANDS AWAY
SHE RUBBED MY LEG WITH HER FOOT UNDER THE TABLE
I CRACKED A JOKE AND SHE TRIED TO PINCH ME WITH HER TOES BUT MY JEANS SAVED ME
FRUSTRATED LOOK
SHE STARTED TO KNIT BUT HER ARTHRITIS WAS BOTHERING HER
FUCK
MAYBE YOU NEED A TALISMAN DRAWN ON...
WILL YOU DRAW A BUNNY?

DRAWING GAVE US AN EXCUSE TO HOLD HANDS
I DREW ALOT OF BUNNIES
THEN I PULLED HER LEG ONTO MY LAP. I WONDERED IF HE COULD SEE HER TOES STICKING UP
WE DIDN'T LEAVE UNTIL ALMOST FOUR
SHOTGUN
BACK AT HER APARTMENT OUR FRIEND SAT DOWN TO DRAW MORE
UM, CAN I TAKE A SHOWER BEFORE I GO?
WHAT COLOR TOWEL DO YOU WANT?
UM..
SHE CRANES HER NECK
5'11"
5'3"

PEACH
WHICH SHAMPOO DID YOU USE?
UM, THE BROWN ONE
THAT'S MINE.
I SHOULD GET GOING.
I'LL WALK YOU DOWN
HUG SUPER TIGHT
I'LL CALL YOU WHEN I GET BACK..
DRAW BACK THEN KISS, HANDS ON HEAD
DRIVE HOME SAFE.
HAVE A GOOD TRIP.
IN THE REARVIEW I WATCH HER CLOSING THE GATE

THE FIRST DAY OF AUTUMN

SEPTEMBER 23

SO...
BLAH BLAH BLAH
BLAH BLAH BLAH
AND...
HEE HEE
HA
RIGHT NOW I WANT TO REACH ACROSS THE TABLE AND MOVE YOUR HAIR
I THINK I'M GOING TO GO FOR A WALK.

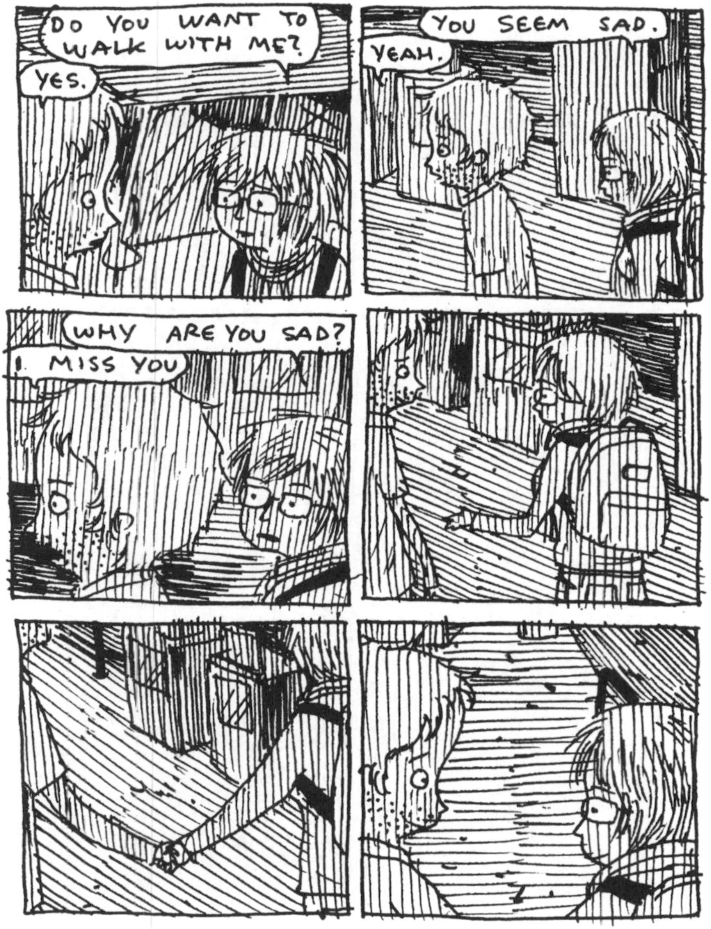
DO YOU WANT TO WALK WITH ME?
YES.
YOU SEEM SAD.
YEAH.
WHY ARE YOU SAD?
I. MISS YOU

WALK WALK TALK WALK
WALK TALK WALK
WALK TALK TALK
WALK WALK
WALK TALK WALK
TALK WALK
WALK TALK TALK
WALK WALK
FINALLY...
DON'T BE SAD, JEFFREY
HUG
ON THE WAY HOME IT POURED RAIN
I WONDERED IF SHE WAS WALKING THROUGH THE RAIN. I WISHED I COULD'VE TAKEN HER HOME

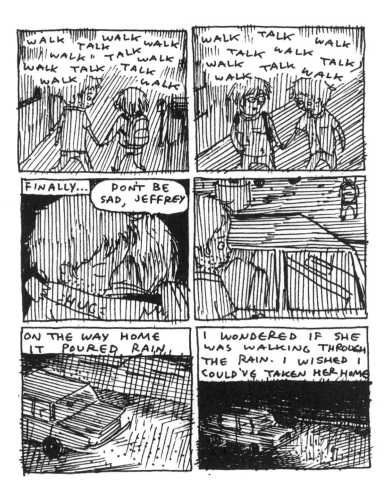

EVERYTHING WILL WORK ITSELF OUT ONE DAY BUT NOT ALL IN ONE DAY

OCTOBER 1

I'M SORRY. I'VE BEEN SICK SINCE FRIDAY. I HAVEN'T CALLED ANYONE. I DIDN'T REALIZE IT WAS SUCH A BIG DEAL.
...
WELL, DO YOU WANT TO HANG OUT TONIGHT OR NOT? BECAUSE I'D LIKE TO
OKAY
PICK HER UP AT HER APARTMENT
HI
HI
HOW WAS ROSHOSHONA?
GOOD..
YOUR HAIR'S DARK..
YEAH. I CHANGED IT FRIDAY..
THANKS

DO YOU WANT A BITE?
NO THANKS
SHE TALKED ALOT AND I SAT THERE TRYING TO SORT OUT THOUGHTS
WE PLAYED TWO GAMES OF SCRABBLE. I WON BOTH.
THEN SHE WAS KNITTING I WATCHED HER KNIT. HER HANDS WERE MOVING SO FAST.
THE DRIVE HOME AND I DON'T SAY ANYTHING.
JEFFREY, ARE YOU EVEN REMOTELY OKAY?
NO
DO YOU WANT TO TALK?
YES

DO YOU WANT TO TALK IN THE CAR, OR...?
YEAH.
MAYBE WE SHOULD PARK SOMEWHERE ELSE... THAT COP THINKS WE'RE SUSPICIOUS
I DON'T KNOW WHERE TO START.
I THOUGHT LAST WEEK WAS SO GOOD, AND THEN YOU DON'T CALL, AND I DON'T KNOW WHAT YOU'RE THINKING
I THINK YOU'RE AWESOME JEFFREY. I WOULDN'T HURT YOU INTENTIONALLY.
WHAT DO YOU WANT FROM ME?

I WANT TO SPEND TIME WITH YOU. I JUST WISH WE COULD FIND SOME SORT OF COMPROMISE WHERE THIS WOULD WORK..
I'M TRYING NOT TO HAVE SO MANY EXPECTATIONS OF YOU. I JUST DON'T FEEL LIKE WE'RE BEING JUST FRIENDS..
THAT'S A BIG DIFFERENCE BETWEEN US. I'M JUST ABLE TO APPROACH US FROM A DIFFERENT PERSPECTIVE..
MAYBE WE DID THINGS BACKWARDS. WE DID THINGS TOO SOON.
I'M NOT GOING TO ARGUE WITH YOU THERE.
...AND THEN THE NIGHT I GOT HOME FROM BETHESDA AND YOU WERE SO... COLD TO ME...
I WAS BEING CAUTIOUS, JEFFREY..
YOU NEVER HESITATE TO POINT OUT HOW I FUCK UP, JEFFREY. I KNOW I CAN BE A FLAKE AND THAT'S NOT A GOOD QUALITY..

I JUST FEEL LIKE I NEED TO RIDE THIS OUT AND IT'LL WORK ITSELF OUT. I FEEL LIKE IM COMING FROM A MUCH BETTER PLACE..
I MEAN, EVER SINCE... SINCE MATT PASSED AWAY..I..
DANIELLE...
IT WAS SO NICE TO TALK TO HER. SO NICE TO HOLD HER HAND...
THE OTHER DAY I TOOK A NAP WITH MY BUNNY AND I THOUGHT THIS WOULD BE SO MUCH BETTER WITH JEFFREY

IT ALMOST TWO. WE SHOULD PROBABLY GO..
YEAH.
CAN I WALK YOU TO YOUR HOUSE?
YES.
AREN'T YOU COLD? WHERE'S YOUR COAT?
I'M FAMOUS FOR NOT WEARING A COAT.
YOU SHOULD WEAR A COAT.

I MISS SNUGGLING WITH YOU
SQUEEZE
JEFFREY, I NEED TO STOP HUGGING YOU OR I'M GOING TO WANT TO KISS YOUR NECK.
GOOD NIGHT JEFFREY BROWN
GOOD NIGHT
I FEEL BETTER WALKING TO THE CAR BUT I STILL FEEL SO CONFLICTED

SOME SONGS ARE HARDER TO LISTEN TO BECAUSE THEY REMIND ME OF YOU.
I WONDER IF IT'S THE SAME FOR YOU.
OR MAYBE THERE'S SONGS YOU LIKE BECAUSE OF THE MEMORIES THEY BRING, OF ME.
HEY, WHAT'RE YOU DOING?
SCANNING AND DRAWING.
ARE YOU HUNGRY? JOHN AND I WERE GONNA GET LUNCH.
WHERE ARE YOU GOING?
WHITE CASTLE.
UMM... OKAY
WE'LL PICK YOU UP IN TEN MINUTES.
OKAY.

TIME HAS A WAY OF DIMINISHING MEMORIES.
I'VE ONLY EATEN AT WHITE CASTLE ONCE. IT WAS A BAD EXPERIENCE.
DETAILS GET FUZZY. ENTIRE PARTS DISAPPEAR.
IT TOOK AN HOUR AND A HALF, BUT WE COULDN'T GET OUT OF THE DRIVE-THROUGH BECAUSE THERE WAS A BARRIER.
YOU'RE LEFT WITH THE FEW THINGS YOU THINK ABOUT AGAIN AND AGAIN.
AND THEN THEY WOULDN'T GIVE US OUR CHANGE.
EVEN THOSE BECOME SOMETHING ELSE EVENTUALLY.
DOES SOMEONE WANT TO SPLIT A TEN PACK?
WE COULD GET A TWENTY PACK, THAT'D BE CHEAPER.
SO I GOT THE UNOFFICIAL WORD THAT THEY'RE GIVING ME THE FULL-TIME POSITION.
THAT'S AWESOME.
I THINK I'M GOING TO GO TO VEGAS TO CELEBRATE, BECAUSE THE NEXT UFC* IS THERE..
THAT'D BE COOL
*ULTIMATE FIGHTING CHAMPIONSHIP

I'M GONNA HELP JOHN GET THE FOOD.
FROMTHATSHIT
TOSS
KICK YOUR FUCKIN' ASS, BITCH!
UM..

I THINK WE HAVE TO MOVE.
WHOSE COAT IS THAT?
I DON'T KNOW. SOME GUY.
DIDN'T HE SEE YOU WERE SITTING THERE?
I DONT THINK IT MATTERED.
ARE THERE ONIONS ON ALL OF THESE? THESE'LL GO RIGHT THROUGH ME
THAT'S WHY THEY'RE CALLED 'SLIDERS'
SOMETIMES ENTIRE DAYS GO BY WITHOUT A SINGLE THOUGHT OF YOU.

EVERY GIRL IS THE END OF THE WORLD FOR ME

DECEMBER 26 2003 - JANUARY 15 2004

GUIDE TO GIRLS
APPEARING IN THIS BOOK (IN ORDER OF APPEARANCE)
ALLISYN
MY FIRST GIRLFRIEND, ALSO MY FIRST EX-GIRLFRIEND
LISA
A FRIEND AND PEN PAL FROM ALABAMA
NICOLE
A FRIEND FROM WORK
DANIELLE
A GIRL I HAD DATED A FEW MONTHS EARLIER BUT HAD MANAGED TO STAY FRIENDS WITH
STEPHANIE
A FRIEND FROM THE COFFEEHOUSE WHERE I GO TO DRAW

CIARA
A GIRL WHO I MEET AT NICOLE'S PARTY
MICHELLE
AN OLD FRIEND FROM MY HOMETOWN GRAND RAPIDS WHO ALSO LIVES IN CHICAGO NOW
THU
A FRIEND AND FORMER HOUSEMATE FROM WHEN I STILL LIVED IN GRAND RAPIDS
JENNIFER
GIRLFRIEND (NOW WIFE) OF MY FRIEND JEREMY
NOT APPEARING
IN THIS BOOK ARE TWO ADDITIONAL GIRLS: CHRISTINE, WIFE OF MY FRIEND AND COLLEGE ROOM-MATE MIKE, AND THEIR DAUGHTER, MORGAN. AT THE TIME OF THESE EVENTS I WAS LIVING IN THEIR ATTIC.
SINCE NEITHER CHRISTINE OR MORGAN ARE ANY SORT OF 'END OF THE WORLD FOR ME', I DECIDED TO NOT INCLUDE THEM, EXCEPT FOR RIGHT HERE

PREVIOUSLY

IN EARLY DECEMBER I GOT AN EMAIL FROM AN OLD FRIEND FROM MY HOMETOWN ABOUT A BOOK I WROTE ABOUT MY FIRST GIRLFRIEND ALLISYN
[YEAH, I WONDER WHAT SHE THINKS ABOUT WHAT I WROTE..]
TAK TAK TAK TAK TAK TAK TAK
[OR IF SHE'S EVEN SEEN THE BOOK]

I DON'T KNOW IF SHE'S READ IT... I CAN FIND OUT THOUGH. I'LL GET HER NUMBER FOR YOU...
D'OH!
AFTER LOSING MY VIRGINITY TO ALLISYN, SHE BROKE MY HEART (NATURALLY) AND AFTER THAT I MOVED TO CHICAGO
I HADN'T SPOKEN TO HER SINCE. I WROTE A LETTER TO HER ONCE, BUT DIDN'T HEAR BACK FROM HER.
OH WELL
IT HAD BEEN THREE YEARS
FW: RE: 'UNLIKELY'
MY NAME IS ALLISYN AND I BELIEVE I AM THE GIRL FROM THE BOOK. I AM TRYING TO GET IN TOUCH WITH JEFFREY BROWN. HERE IS MY PHONE NUMBER...

FRIDAY
DECEMBER 26

DECEMBER
BIP
BEEP
BOOP
BEEP
BEEP
HI. THIS IS JEFF
HI. HOW ARE YOU?
GOOD. UM, HOW ARE YOU?
GOOD.
SO, DO YOU STILL WANT TO HANG OUT?
YEAH. HOW DO I GET THERE?
UH-HUH. OKAY. UH-HUH. OKAY, I THINK I'VE GOT IT..
I'M NERVOUS.
WHY?
BECAUSE I HAVEN'T SEEN HER IN THREE AND A HALF YEARS
SO? YOU'VE HAD SEX WITH HER. HOW CAN YOU BE NERVOUS?

WHAT'S SHE WANT FROM YOU, ANYWAY?
I DUNNO.
WHAT DO YOU WANT FROM IT?
I DUNNO. TO BE FRIENDS.
IS THIS IT?
SHIT, I HAVE TO TURN AROUND..

KNOCK
KNOCK
KNOCK
2B
HI.
HI. COME IN
WHAT'S SO FUNNY?
IT'S JUST WEIRD TO SEE YOU.
WHY?
SHRUG
DID YOU FIND YOUR WAY OKAY?
UM, YEAH

SOON...
...AND THAT'S WHEN I KIND OF HIT BOTTOM I GUESS AND I MOVED OUT IN THE MIDDLE OF THE NIGHT...
COUGH (AHEM)
YEAH
SORRY I WAS SUCH A BITCH TO YOU.
IT'S OKAY. I DON'T THINK YOU WERE THAT BAD REALLY.
THE KITTIES LIKE YOU.
YEAH
COUGH
MEW
DO YOU WANT SOME LEMONADE?
YAY!
SURE.
UM, DO YOU MIND IF I SMOKE?
COUGH
NO.
THANKS
I'M GOING TO QUIT. MY FRIENDS SAY IF I'M GOING TO BE HANGING OUT WITH YOU, I'LL HAVE TO QUIT FOR SURE.
HEH

MY FRIENDS LIKE YOU. FROM WHAT THEY KNOW, ANYWAY.
THAT'S GOOD
COUGH COUGH
YOUR FRIENDS DON'T LIKE ME, DO THEY?
UMMM... THEY DON'T REALLY KNOW YOU
THIS IS MY NEW CAMERA I GOT FOR CHRISTMAS. I'D TAKE PICTURES OF US HANGING OUT IF I KNEW HOW TO USE IT...
COUGH COUGH
YEP.
YOU'RE GIVING ME THE CRAZY LOOK..
SORRY
COUGH
IT'S JUST WEIRD SEEING YOU AGAIN.
I'M MUCH DIFFERENT NOW, YOU KNOW
YEAH

SATURDAY DECEMBER 27

IT'S FOUR O'CLOCK... I SHOULD REALLY GO
COUGH COUGH
OKAY
ARE YOU GOING TO BE OKAY DRIVING HOME?
YEAH.
COUGH
ARE YOU SURE? YOU COULD SLEEP ON THE COUCH..
I'LL BE OKAY
COUGH
I'M GLAD YOU CAME.
ME TOO.
SQUEEZE
SQUEEZE

DRIVE SAFE
I WILL.
PROMISE?
COUGH COUGH
I WILL. DON'T WORRY.
2B
COUGH COUGH
SORRY, WE DONT ACCEPT BOTTLECAPS
?
JUST KIDDING
OH
FREE 20 OZ
ON YOUR WAY TO WORK?
ENH, ON MY WAY HOME TO CHICAGO... JUST CAME BACK TO VISIT.. FAMILY FOR CHRISTMAS
COUGH
WELL THAT'S GOOD. YOU HAVE A GOOD ONE.
THANKS, YOU TOO
ATM

SUNDAY

DECEMBER 28

HI. IS THIS JEFF?
YEAH.
HI. THIS IS LISA.
HI.
COUGH
SO I'M IN TOWN. ARE YOU STILL FREE FOR COFFEE TONIGHT?
YEAH, DEFINITELY
COUGH COUGH
DO YOU WANT TO MEET ME AT EARWAX?
OKAY
UM... ARE YOU JEFF?
ARE YOU LISA?
HI
HI
SORRY. I'M A LITTLE NERVOUS, MEETING YOU IN PERSON..
YEAH. ME TOO..
COUGH COUGH COUGH
SORRY I'M A LITTLE SICK
I INVITED MY FRIEND NICHOLAS WHO I'M HERE WITH. IS THAT OKAY?
YEAH, WE CAN MOVE TO A BIGGER TABLE WHEN HE GETS HERE..
...AND THEN I WENT BACK TO SWEDEN...
..SO, DO YOU DRAW ALL THE TIME?
ETC
TAKE A PICTURE?
COUGH
ETC ETC
...WORKING FULL TIME STILL, BUT

MONDAY

DECEMBER 29

SURE. HOW DO I GET TO YOUR HOUSE?
I'LL DRAW YOU A MAP.
COUGH COUGH
SEE?
THERE'S ME, AND THERE'S MY DOGS...
RING RING
HELLO?
HI JEFFREY. IT'S DANIELLE
HI. I HAVENT HEARD FROM YOU IN A WHILE. HOW ARE YOU?
COUGH
GOOD. I'VE BEEN GOOD. HEY, DO YOU WANT TO HANG OUT SOMETIME THIS WEEK? I'VE GOT A NEW YEAR'S GIFT FOR YOU.

UM, SURE... I'M GOING BACK TO GRAND RAPIDS TONIGHT, BUT... MAYBE.. SATURDAY?
YEAH, SATURDAY'S GOOD. I'LL GIVE YOU A CALL.
OKAY. I'LL TALK TO YOU THEN.
COUGH
ARE YOU STILL COMING INTO TOWN TOMORROW AGAIN? DO YOU WANT TO HANG OUT?
TAK TAK TAK TAK TAK TAK TAK
YEAH. I'M LEAVING TONIGHT. I'LL CALL YOU TOMORROW NIGHT
TUESDAY
DECEMBER 30
YOU'RE GOING TO HANG OUT WITH HER AGAIN?
YEAH
COUGH
IS IT A DATE?
NO.

WE'RE JUST FRIENDS.
BE CAREFUL.
COUGH COUGH
I AM. WHY?
IT'S HARD FOR PEOPLE TO CHANGE.
SHE'S CHANGED ALOT THOUGH.
ALL I'M SAYING IS BE CAREFUL.
OKAY.
HEY
HI.
SO, UM, DO YOU STILL WANT TO HANG OUT AGAIN TONIGHT?
YEAH, DEFINITELY.
OKAY, I'LL BE OVER IN A LITTLE BIT.
COUGH COUGH

HI.
HI.
SO WHERE DO YOU WANNA EAT?
I DUNNO. YOU KNOW THE RESTRAUNTS AROUND HERE BETTER
UMM...
HOW ABOUT OLIVE GARDEN?
COUGH
OKAY
GRAND RAPIDS HAS CHANGED A LOT...
DID YOU SEE THE WEATHERBALL'S OVER HERE NOW?
HUH.. I HAD TOTALLY FORGOTTEN ABOUT THE WEATHERBALL.
SO WHAT DOES DAN HAVE TO SAY ABOUT YOU HANGING OUT WITH ME?
GIGGLE
WHAT?
UM, I CAN'T SAY
DOES HE HATE ME AS MUCH AS YOU HATE KATE?
UM, I DONT THINK SO
COUGH

Y'KNOW, IF YOU PAY FOR DINNER, THIS IS A DATE.
I WAS GOING TO PAY FOR DINNER ANYWAY.
STILL.
THANKS
I DON'T HAVE TO GO TO WORK UNTIL TEN. DO YOU WANT TO HANG OUT UNTIL THEN?
SURE
SO WHAT EXACTLY DO YOU DO FOR WORK, ANYWAY?
COUGH
I WATCH OVER KIDS. IT'S KIND OF LIKE A HALF-WAY HOME. I HAVE TO COUNSEL A LITTLE..

I HAD MY DOCTOR APPOINTMENT TODAY. HE GAVE ME NEW BIRTH CONTROL TO TRY. IT'S GOT ALL KINDS OF CRAZINESS TO IT.. I CAN SHOW YOU IF YOU WANT.
UM, OKAY
..AND HERE'S THE TIMER...I THINK I MIGHT'VE BROKE IT THOUGH. IT'S WEIRD BECAUSE I HAVEN'T HAD SEX IN A LONG TIME..
COUGH COUGH COUGH
HEY, WAIT, TURN AROUND, YOU'VE GOT A NEW TATOO...
COUGH
YEP. I HAD DRAGONS ADDED..
YEAH..
IS IT RAISED AT ALL?
UM, A LITTLE

THIS IS THE NEW TRIVIA PURSUIT I GOT FOR CHRISTMAS. IT'S ALL ABOUT THE 80'S, SO I'LL TOTALLY DEFEAT YOU THIS TIME.
HEY, I WAS ALIVE IN THE 80'S TOO
COUGH
WE'LL HAVE TO PLAY THE NEXT TIME WE HANG OUT
OKAY.
SO, CAN YOU VISIT AGAIN?
MAYBE... I'VE GOT SOME VACATION DAYS AND STUFF TO USE BY MARCH...
COUGH
YEAH. WITH WORK AND SCHOOL, I'VE PROBABLY GOT LESS TIME THAN YOU. NOT THAT YOU'RE NOT BUSY.
I KNOW WHAT YOU MEAN
BUT I'M GOING TO CHICAGO WITH MY FRIENDS NEAR THE END OF JANUARY SO I CAN COME VISIT YOU THEN.
YEAH?
YEAH.

THEY'LL BE OKAY BY THEMSELVES, AND THEN WE CAN HANG OUT.
OKAY.
COUGH COUGH
I SHOULD PROBABLY GET GOING TO WORK.
YEAH... I SHOULD GET GOING TOO. I'M STILL SICK.
2B
I'M REALLY GLAD YOU CAME OVER AGAIN.
ME TOO

SMECK
SMECK
KISS
KISS
KISS
KISS

OKAY. I HAVE TO GO
OKAY
COUGH
HI. I HAD A REALLY NICE TIME TONIGHT.
I HOPE YOU DIDNT MIND THAT I KISSED YOU..
TAK TAK TAK TAK
[NO, THE KISS WAS FINE. IT WAS NICE...

WEDNESDAY

DECEMBER 31

ARE YOU GOING TO KISS HER?
NO. WE'RE JUST FRIENDS.
SHE'S GOING TO WANT A KISS.
SHE WOULDN'T CALL AT THE LAST MINUTE. SHE EXPECTS YOU TO KISS HER..
YEAH, AT MIDNIGHT. YOU HAVE TO.
BYE
HI. I'VE STILL GOT A LITTLE MORE TO DO TO GET READY.
YOU'RE NEVER READY ON TIME
COUGH
I HUNG OUT WITH ALLISYN AGAIN LAST NIGHT. SHE KISSED ME.
DID YOU KISS HER BACK?
YOU DID, DIDN'T YOU?
OKAY, LET'S GO
COUGH
OKAY
WHAT TIME IS IT?
UM, IT'S TEN TO MIDNIGHT.
SHOOT!
WE'LL STILL MAKE IT

HI
THIS IS MY FRIEND JEFFREY
HI
HI
HERE, CAN YOU OPEN IT?
UM, SURE
SIX
FIVE
FOUR
OOH, HURRY
THREE
TWO
POP
ONE
HAPPY NEW YEAR!
PECK!

WE WERE IN DRUM CORPS TOGETHER..
COUGH
OH
C'MON, GUYS!
DANCE!
ERM
AFTER SOME "DANCING"
WHAT'S WRONG?
RUB RUB RUB RUB RUB
THERE'S SOMETHING IN MY EYE..
RUB RUB RUB RUB
WELL STOP POKING AT IT
NO
GO TO THE BATHROOM AND WASH IT OUT
RUB RUB

IT'S ALL RED BUT I DON'T SEE ANYTHING...
DON'T POKE AT IT ANYMORE!
OKAY
...AND I USED TO GO ALL OVER THE COUNTRY COMPETING. ONE YEAR WE FINISHED REALLY HIGH...
UH-HUNH
HEY DO YOU WANT TO WATCH MY DRUM CORPS VIDEO?
OKAY
COUGH
THIS IS FUNNY. YOU REALLY DO NEED TO SEE 'DRUM LINE'.
SHH, LOOK THERE'S ME!
COUGH
...AND MY MOM JUST DOESN'T GET THAT I DON'T HAVE THE TIME...
YEAH
YAWN
I'M TIRED. WHAT TIME IS IT?
OH GEEZ, IT'S THREE

THURSDAY

JANUARY 1

COUGH COUGH
I HAVE TO HURRY...
COUGH
COUGH
YAWN
I'M A SLUT. I KISSED TWO GIRLS IN THE PAST TWO NIGHTS.
HEE HEE

FRIDAY

JANUARY 2

YEAH, IT WAS GOOD.
COUGH
HAVE A SAFE TRIP HOME.
THANKS.
BYE
BYE
COUGH COUGH
JEFFREY! YOU MADE IT. COME IN.
HI

HEY EVERYBODY, THIS IS MY FRIEND JEFFREY. WHAT DO YOU WANT TO DRINK? YOU HAVE TO HAVE A DRINK.
UM, OKAY... A REALLY WEAK SCREWDRIVER
I'M GONNA MAKE SOME PANCAKES. DOES ANYONE ELSE WANT PANCAKES?
JEFF, DO YOU WANT PANCAKES?
NO THANKS
THAT DOESN'T EVEN LOOK LIKE AN IGLOO!
WELL, HOW WOULD YOU MAKE ONE?
LIKE THIS..
COUGH
OH YEAH
DO YOU GO BY 'JEFF,' OR 'JEFFREY'?
EITHER ONE.
HM. 'JEFFREY BROWN.'
COUGH
WAIT, DO YOU DO COMICS?
YEAH.

SATURDAY

JANUARY 3

OH, IT'S YOU.
SOMEONE TOLD ME I HAD ANOTHER TABLE AND I SAID 'OH NO' BUT NOW I'M HAPPY.
COUGH
COF
HI
HI
HERE.
IT'S YOUR NEW YEAR'S GIFT
THANKS!
COUGH COUGH
YOU'RE WELCOME

CAN I GET YOU SOMETHING?
JUST COFFEE
...AND THEN SHE YELLS AT ME, WHEN IT WASN'T EVEN MY PROJECT TO TAKE CARE OF...
THAT SUCKS.
SO WHAT HAVE YOU BEEN WORKING ON NOW?
I JUST FINISHED THIS ONE STORY AND NOW I'VE GOT TO WORK ON THIS OTHER BOOK, MY SUPER-HERO THING..
ARE YOU READY TO GO?
YEAH
COUGH
DO YOU WANT A RIDE HOME?
SURE.

THANKS FOR THE CD. IT WAS GOOD TO SEE YOU
YOU'RE WELCOME
YOU SMELL NICE.
REALLY? THANKS...I'M NOT WEARING ANYTHING THOUGH..
REALLY? YOU STILL SMELL NICE..
SQUEEZE
BYE
BYE JEFFREY

SUNDAY

JANUARY 4

WHAT?!
BEEN SEEIN
SOMEONE EL
FUCK!
TAK TAK TAK TAK
TAK TAK TAK TAK
TAK TAK TAK
TAK
DELETE
TAK TAK TAK TAK
TAK TAK
DELETE
TAK TAK TAK
TAK TAK
TAK TAK
DELETE
COUGH
COUGH
[I DON'T GET YOU. WHY DIDN'T YOU TELL ME THIS? THIS REALLY SUCKS. I FEEL LIKE AN IDIOT...]
TAK
TAK
TAK
TAK
TAK
TAK
TAK

HEY STEPHANIE, THIS IS JEFF... UM, GIVE ME A CALL LATER IF YOU HAVE A CHANCE..
COUGH COUGH
COUGH COUGH COUGH
RINGGG RINGGG
HELLO?
HI. IT'S STEPHANIE
HI
SO WHAT'S UP?
WELL, I GOT A CRAPPY EMAIL FROM ALLISYN...
YEAH?

MONDAY

JANUARY 5

FURIOUS EMAIL EXCHANGE!
I DIDN'T MEAN FOR IT TO HAPPEN. IT JUST DID. AND YOU KEPT TALKING ABOUT BEING FRIENDS FIRST..
TAK TAK TAK TAK TAK
[AND THIS IS EXACTLY WHY I WANTED TO BE CAUTIOUS. YOU COULD'VE AT LEAST TOLD ME BEFORE KISSING ME]
WE NEVER DISCUSSED BEING EXCLUSIVE. AND I MET HIM AFTER WE KISSED, AT MY FRIEND'S NEW YEAR'S DINNER
TAK TAK TAK TAK TAK TAK
[DON'T YOU THINK YOU'D WANT TO DISCUSS EXCLUSIVITY BEFORE YOU GO AND START SEEING SOMEONE ELSE?]
I DON'T UNDERSTAND WHY YOU'RE SO UPSET. I TELL HIM ABOUT YOU, I TELL YOU ABOUT HIM, BUT SUDDENLY I'M THE WHORE OF BABYLON?
TAK TAK TAK TAK
[YEAH, BUT HE KNEW ABOUT ME BEFOREHAND, I HAD TO FIND OUT AFTERWARD. I WAS PRETTY MUCH IN LOVE WITH YOU AT FIRST SIGHT, THEN YOU DISAPPEAR, THEN SOMEHOW I END UP WITH YOU AND YOU BREAK MY HEART...]
[... SO I SPEND YEARS GETTING OVER YOU, FINALLY ACCEPT THAT I'M NEVER GOING TO SEE YOU AGAIN, AND THEN SUDDENLY WE'RE BACK IN TOUCH AND IT'S GREAT AND YOU KISS ME AND THE NEXT DAY YOU START SEEING SOMEONE ELSE?]
TAK TAK TAK TAK TAK TAK TAK TAK
I'M SORRY I HURT YOU. I REALLY DIDN'T MEAN TO. YOU'RE A WONDERFUL PERSON OR ELSE I NEVER WOULD'VE LOVED YOU. I UNDERSTAND IF YOU HATE ME NOW.

WHAT'S WRONG?
I'M SAD.
WHY?
BECAUSE OF THE WHOLE ALLISYN THING.
I'M SAD TOO.
WHY ARE YOU SAD?
COUGH COUGH
THERE'S THIS BOY, AND, UM... LESSEE, I'M TRYING TO BE VAGUE HERE...
I KIND OF HAVE AN UNREASONABLE CRUSH ON HIM. LIKE, I SHOULDN'T, BUT I DO...

AND I KNOW I SHOULDN'T BE BOTHERED BY IT, BUT HE'S BEEN SPENDING TIME WITH THIS GIRL..
IS SHE TALKING ABOUT ME?!
TAP TAP TAP
HEY STEPHANIE
HM?
DO YOU WANT TO SEE DRUMLINE SOMETIME?
YOU'VE ALREADY SEEN IT THOUGH.
YEAH. BUT I HAVEN'T SEEN IT WITH YOU.
UM, OKAY.

TUESDAY

JANUARY 6

WEDNESDAY

JANUARY 7

HI JEFFREY
HI
CAN I COUNT MY MONEY AT YOUR TABLE?
SURE.
I FINISHED KNITTING THE SCARF FOR MY FRIEND. I'M STARTING TO KNIT A LITTLE HAT NOW.
YEAH.
I HAVE TO GO CATCH MY TRAIN.
YEAH
I'M DONE DRAWING DO YOU WANT SOME COMPANY?

I CAN GIVE YOU A RIDE HOME, IF YOU WANT.
REALLY? ARE YOU SURE?
SURE. I HAVE TO GO WEST TO GET HOME ANYWAY.
OKAY.
WOOP!
CAREFUL...
COUGH
HAVE YOU EVER BEEN ICE SKATING?
NOT REALLY.
WE SHOULD GO SOMETIME.
OKAY.
THERE'S A PLACE RIGHT DOWNTOWN WHERE WE COULD GO.
YEAH.

THANKS FOR THE RIDE, JEFFREY
BYE
THURSDAY
JANUARY 8
RING
RING

HELLO?
HI JEFF
HI STEPHANIE
I HAVE A QUESTION FOR YOU...
YEAH?
IN PAUL'S COMIC, THE SECOND ISSUE IS THE FIRST PART OF A STORY, BUT IT DOESN'T CONTINUE THE STUFF FROM THE FIRST ISSUE?
RIGHT. ISSUES 2, 3 AND 4 ARE ALL ONE STORY, AND ISSUE 1 IS ALL IT'S OWN THING..
OKAY. THAT'S WHAT I THOUGHT
ANYWAY, I GOTTA GO. 'MUST SEE TV' IS ABOUT TO START.
MAYBE WE CAN HANG OUT SOON AND TALK MORE ABOUT PAUL'S COMICS.
OKAY. BYE.

FRIDAY

JANUARY 9

COUGH COUGH
HAHA! DUDE YOU ARE SO DRUNK
C'MON, WE CAN WATCH FROM UPSTAIRS
OKAY.
COUGH COUGH
RUB RUB RUB
IT'S REALLY PRETTY OUT
YEAH.
COUGH
UM, CAN I USE YOUR SHOWER?
OF COURSE..

YOUR SHOWER'S STILL NOT FIXED YET?!
NO...
(MY SHOWER, SEPT. THROUGH JAN.)
THANKS. I NEEDED THAT.
NO PROBLEM JEFFREY
LEWIS REALLY NEEDS TO PLAY MORE. HE'S SO GOOD.
YEAH. I'M GLAD I WENT
COUGH
BLAH BLAH BLAH BLAH BLAH BLAH
COUGH
BLAH BLAH BLAH BLAH BLAH BLAH

SATURDAY

JANUARY 10

WHAT ARE YOU UP TO?
I MOVED HERE FOR SCHOOL. AND I'M MARRIED NOW.
HOLY COW. REALLY?
WHAT ABOUT YOU? DO YOU HAVE A GIRLFRIEND YET?
DO YOU REMEMBER THAT GIRL ALLISYN? I DATED HER RIGHT AFTER YOU MOVED.
WHAT HAPPENED?
WELL, SHE BROKE MY HEART. BUT SHE JUST GOT BACK IN TOUCH WITH ME AND WE HUNG OUT AND SHE KISSED ME AND THE NEXT DAY STARTED SEEING SOMEONE ELSE..
NO!
JEFF, DO YOU LIKE VIETNAMESE GIRLS?
UM, I DUNNO. I DON'T DISLIKE THEM. I WOULDN'T SAY I LIKE THEM SPECIFICALLY. I DON'T REALLY KNOW ANY VIETNAMESE GIRLS BESIDES YOU..
OH, 'CAUSE I HAVE A FRIEND. SHE'S A DESIGNER AND SHE'S PRETTY SMART...
UM, OKAY

SUNDAY

JANUARY 11

THIS PIZZA IS REALLY GOOD, JEREMY
THANKS
HEY, WE'RE GOING TO SEE KELLY HOGAN AT THE HIDEOUT ON WEDNESDAY. DO YOU WANT TO GO?
UM, PROBABLY NOT..
WHY NOT?
UM, THAT'S ONE OF THE DAYS I USUALLY GO TO EARWAX BECAUSE IT'S ONE OF THE DAYS STEPHANIE WORKS..
GIGGLE
WHAT?
NOTHING. IT'S CUTE

MONDAY

JANUARY 12

TUESDAY

JANUARY 13

UM, CAN I GET A COFFEE?
WITH VANILLA?
YES
HEE HEE
SO DID YOU HEAR FROM THAT GIRL YOU WERE HANGING OUT WITH?
UM, NO
I MEAN, SHE STARTED SEEING SOMEONE ELSE THE DAY AFTER SHE KISSED ME..
WHAT?! I DIDN'T KNOW THAT.
YEAH. IT SUCKS.
SHE PLAYED YOU!

WEDNESDAY

JANUARY 14

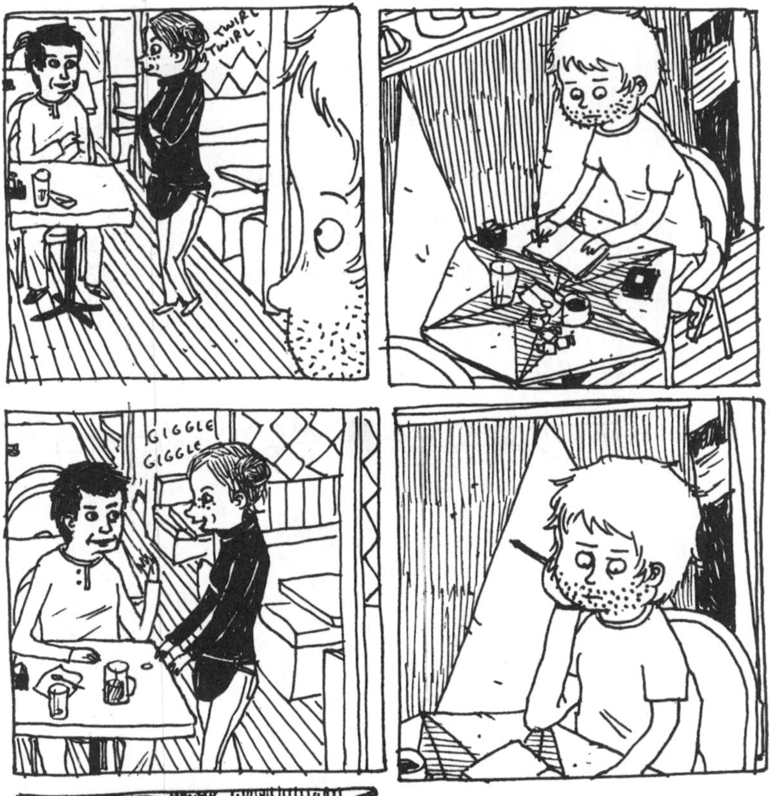

THURSDAY

JANUARY 15

EET EET EET EET EET EE
BEEP
HEY, DO YOU WANT TO TAKE YOUR LUNCH BREAK WITH ME?
SURE.
OKAY. CAN YOU TAKE IT NOW?
WHERE DO YOU WANT TO GO?
HOW ABOUT CHIPOTLE?
YEAH, THAT SOUNDS GOOD.
ARE YOU STILL SAD?
YEAH.

YOU KNOW WHAT YOU NEED TO DO?
YOU NEED TO JUST USE A GIRL..
HEE HEE
YEAH...
FIN

EPILOGUE

ONE YEAR LATER

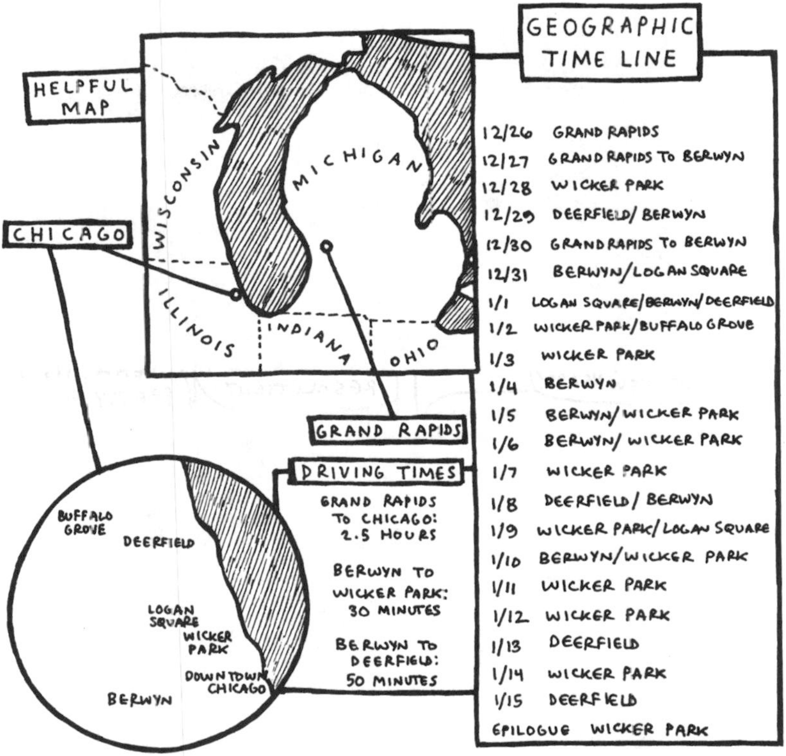
GEOGRAPHIC TIME LINE
HELPFUL MAP
WISCONSIN
MICHIGAN
ILLINOIS
INDIANA
OHIO
CHICAGO
GRAND RAPIDS
BUFFALO GROVE
DEERFIELD
LOGAN SQUARE
WICKER PARK
DOWNTOWN CHICAGO
BERWYN
DRIVING TIMES
GRAND RAPIDS TO CHICAGO: 2.5 HOURS
BERWYN TO WICKER PARK: 30 MINUTES
BERWYN TO DEERFIELD: 50 MINUTES
12/26 GRAND RAPIDS
12/27 GRAND RAPIDS TO BERWYN
12/28 WICKER PARK
12/29 DEERFIELD/ BERWYN
12/30 GRAND RAPIDS TO BERWYN
12/31 BERWYN/LOGAN SQUARE
1/1 LOGAN SQUARE/BERWYN/DEERFIELD
1/2 WICKER PARK/BUFFALO GROVE
1/3 WICKER PARK
1/4 BERWYN
1/5 BERWYN/ WICKER PARK
1/6 BERWYN/ WICKER PARK
1/7 WICKER PARK
1/8 DEERFIELD/ BERWYN
1/9 WICKER PARK/ LOGAN SQUARE
1/10 BERWYN/WICKER PARK
1/11 WICKER PARK
1/12 WICKER PARK
1/13 DEERFIELD
1/14 WICKER PARK
1/15 DEERFIELD
EPILOGUE WICKER PARK

REALITY IN TV IS AWESOMMMMMMMME!

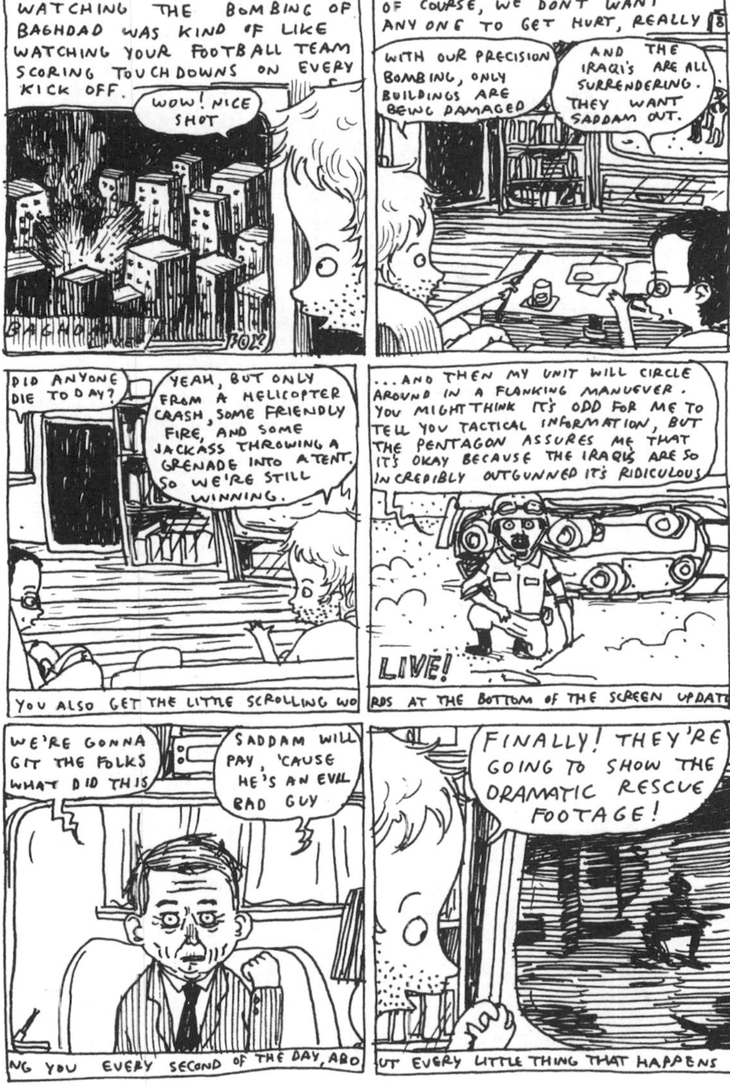
WATCHING THE BOMBING OF BAGHDAD WAS KIND OF LIKE WATCHING YOUR FOOTBALL TEAM SCORING TOUCHDOWNS ON EVERY KICK OFF.
WOW! NICE SHOT
OF COURSE, WE DON'T WANT ANYONE TO GET HURT, REALLY
WITH OUR PRECISION BOMBING, ONLY BUILDINGS ARE BEING DAMAGED
AND THE IRAQI'S ARE ALL SURRENDERING. THEY WANT SADDAM OUT.
DID ANYONE DIE TODAY?
YEAH, BUT ONLY FROM A HELICOPTER CRASH, SOME FRIENDLY FIRE, AND SOME JACKASS THROWING A GRENADE INTO A TENT. SO WE'RE STILL WINNING.
...AND THEN MY UNIT WILL CIRCLE AROUND IN A FLANKING MANUEVER. YOU MIGHT THINK IT'S ODD FOR ME TO TELL YOU TACTICAL INFORMATION, BUT THE PENTAGON ASSURES ME THAT IT'S OKAY BECAUSE THE IRAQI'S ARE SO INCREDIBLY OUTGUNNED IT'S RIDICULOUS
LIVE!
YOU ALSO GET THE LITTLE SCROLLING WORDS AT THE BOTTOM OF THE SCREEN UPDATI
WE'RE GONNA GIT THE FOLKS WHAT DID THIS
SADDAM WILL PAY, 'CAUSE HE'S AN EVIL BAD GUY
FINALLY! THEY'RE GOING TO SHOW THE DRAMATIC RESCUE FOOTAGE!
NG YOU EVERY SECOND OF THE DAY, ABOUT EVERY LITTLE THING THAT HAPPENS

THAT BATTLE IS ACTUALLY HAPPENING RIGHT NOW! HOW EXCITING!
OOH! BURNING TANKS!
CLAP CLAP CLAP
YOU ALSO GET THE LITTLE SCROLL
ING WORDS AT THE BOTTOM OF THE
THE CLIMAX WAS THE STATUE OF SADDAM BEING TOPPLED - THE ONLY THING THAT COULD'VE MADE IT BETTER WOULD'VE BEEN A PRIME TIME SLOT INSTEAD OF HAPPENING IN THE MORNING.
SCREEN UPDATING YOU EVERY SECO
IT WOULD'VE BEEN A GOOD ENDING IF THIS WAS A MOVIE AND NOT TELEVISION
YAAYY! WE WON!
ND OF THE DAY, ABOUT EVERY
BUT...
WELL, WE HAVEN'T, UM, ACTUALLY FOUND ANY WEAPONS OF MASS DESTRUCTION, YET...
YAWN
LITTLE THING THAT HAPPENS UNTIL YOU
BUT WE DID FIND THIS COOL TRUCK!
REALIZE IT'S JUST REPETITIVE AND YOU

ONCE AGAIN, HERE'S MORE FOOTAGE OF A COOL TRUCK THAT IS SIMILAR TO THE ONE THAT MAY HAVE BEEN FOUND LAST WEEK...
GIVE UP HOPE THAT THERE'S GOI
IT'S HARD NOT TO LOSE INTEREST, I GUESS
LONG HARD SLOG? THEY SHOULD HAVE MENTIONED THAT IN THE PREVIEWS
NG TO BE NEW STUFF TO READ...
FORTUNATELY AMERICA WAS ABLE TO RETREAT INTO THE SECURITY OF IT'S REGULARLY SCHEDULED REALITY TV SHOWS THIS FALL
OOH, SCANTILY CLAD WOMEN
surf surf surf surf surf surf surf stop
PARADISE HOTEL, AMERICAN IDOL, QUEER EYE FOR THE STRAIGHT GUY, TRADING SPACES... NOT TO MENTION CLASSICS LIKE BLIND DATE, COPS, AND PEOPLE'S COURT*... TV FULL OF REAL PEOPLE
DAMMIT! WHY IS CHARLA SUCH A BITCH TO DAVE?
* ACTUALLY I PREFER JUDGE MATHIS
AVERAGE JOE SCHMO MILLIONAIRE
THAT'S... BEAUTIFUL
I'M A SEXY AND TALENTED UNEMPLOYED BACHELOR
I'M A HOT, INTELLIGENT SINGLE WOMAN ABOUT TO ENTER MY SEXUAL PEAK
YAY! NOW WE'VE WON A MILLION DOLLARS AND A RANCH!
sniff
REALITY IS BEST WHEN SLIGHTLY MANIPULATED FOR OUR PLEASURE
I HOPE NEXT SEASON'S WAR HAS A BETTER FINISH

2004 YEAR IN REVIEW
THIS SPRING, I MOVED BACK INTO CHICAGO FROM THE SUBURBS*.
THE BABY'S DUE IN APRIL
I THINK I'M GOING TO GET MY OWN, UM, APARTMENT..
*I WAS LIVING WITH FRIENDS
NOW I WALK TO THE COMICS SHOP AND RECORD STORE
AND THE COFFEE HOUSE WHERE I DRAW COMICS
THIS SPRING I ALSO HAD A LITTLE SPAT WITH MY PUBLISHER
YEAH, BUT YOU SAID FEBRUARY!
"DEMOCRATIC PEOPLES DON'T LIKE TO FIGHT"

DON'T THEY UNDERSTAND WE'RE HELPING THEM?
POW POW POW POW
WE'RE MUCH SAFER NOW. KILLING PEOPLE GIVES THEM LESS MOTIVATION TO ATTACK US.
FORTUNATELY, BUSH WANTS TO DEVELOPE A NEW NUCLEAR WEAPON TO FIGHT THE TERRORISTS
I AM SO PROUD OF MY COUNTRY
WE HAVE THE MOST GOLD, THEREFORE WE ARE THE BEST
ALSO IN SPORTS:
NO HOCKEY SEASON
WE'RE NOT MAKING ENOUGH MILLIONS OF DOLLARS
WE'RE NOT MAKING ENOUGH MILLIONS OF DOLLARS
PLAYER
OWNER
NO ONE CARES MUCH

ECONOMY? THE ECONOMY WON'T SAVE US FROM THE TERRORISTS
WHAT
I KNOW WHAT'S RIGHT, I'M NOT BLINDED BY SCIENCE
I'VE GOT A MANDATE FROM THE PEOPLE*
* HALF OF THEM
THE GREATNESS OF AMERICA KNOWS NO LIMITS!
I TRAVELLED ALOT THIS YEAR
NOV
AUG
NOV
APR
OCT
JUN
MAR
FEB
JUN
JULY
MAY
OCT
OCT
THAT MAY HAVE CONTRIBUTED TO STRESS AT MY DAY JOB...
... AND SO YOU DON'T GET A RAISE THIS YEAR

SEPTEMBER
PAIN
THANK GOD I HAVE INSURANCE
YOU ALSO HAVE ULCERS
WHAT? WHY?
SEPTEMBER: FALL FOR A GIRL
OCTOBER: SHE LEAVES
MUSIC SAVES MY LIFE
THIS IPOD IS GREAT! IT'S LIKE I'M CARRYING AROUND MY ENTIRE CD COLLECTION!
AUGUST
WHAT? WHY ISN'T IT WORKING DAMMIT

SEPTEMBER
FINALLY, MY REPLACEMENT IPOD! WAIT, WHY ISN'T THIS ONE WORKING?
OCTOBER
OKAY, FINALLY, THIS ONE WORKS..
NOVEMBER
WHAT? NOW THIS ONE ISN'T WORKING. I HAVE TO SEND IT BACK AGAIN
DECEMBER
SHE HASN'T WRITTEN IN A WHILE...
WAIT, WHY AM I DISAPPOINTED? I JUST GOT A CHECK FOR DRAWING COMICS!
OTHER THAN WAR AND THE ELECTION, IT'S BEEN A PRETTY GOOD YEAR I GUESS.

THOUGHTS ON NEW ORLEANS (AFTER THE HURRICANE)

I'VE BEEN TO NEW ORLEANS TWICE. BOTH TIMES WERE FOR WEDDINGS, WHICH HAPPENED TO BE A WEEK APART, LAST OCTOBER
BUSH
BUSH
BUSH
THE SECOND OF THE WEDDINGS WAS HELD IN THE CITY, PRECEDED BY THE OBLIGATORY VISIT TO BOURBON STREET
IT WASN'T REALLY MY KIND OF PLACE...
IT JUST SEEMED KIND OF POINTLESS AND DEVOID OF MEANING

THE RECEPTION WAS HELD IN THE NEW ORLEANS AQUARIUM OF THE AMERICAS
WE GOT TO PET A SHARK
AND AT THE RISK OF LOOKING LIKE A COMPLETE MORON, I DANCED.
THE AQUARIUM WAS STRUCTURALLY UNHARMED BY THE STORM, YET ALMOST ALL OF ITS FISH- 6,000 ANIMALS- DIED.
WHILE WATER FLOODED THE CITY, POWER GENERATORS AT THE AQUARIUM FAILED, TAKING AWAY THE ESSENTIAL CIRCULATION OF OXYGEN IN THE WATER PROVIDED BY AIR PUMPS

THE FIRST WEDDING HAD BEEN HELD ACROSS THE BAY IN MANDEVILLE
I HITCHED A RIDE FROM THE AIRPORT WITH A RELATIVE OF THE BRIDE.
Sporty little rental car
WHILE DRIVING ACROSS THE PONTCHARTRAIN CAUSEWAY A PELICAN APPEARED NEXT TO US
HEY LOOK
IT MATCHED OUR SPEED AND FLEW ALONGSIDE US FOR A COUPLE MINUTES
IN MY MEMORY IT TAKES ON MYTHIC SIZE

AFTER THE HURRICANE THERE WERE PICTURES OF THE CAUSEWAY BEING VIRTUALLY GONE
IT TURNED OUT THIS WASN'T THE PONTCHARTRAIN CAUSEWAY, BUT I-10 BRIDGE TO THE EAST
THE PONTCHARTRAIN CAUSEWAY WAS VIRTUALLY UNDAMAGED, AND ALREADY THERE IS TALK OF RE-OPENING THE FRENCH QUARTER...
I HAVE NO CURRENT PLANS TO RETURN.

TO WENATCHEE

REYHOUND
KLAK
KLAK
CAN WE GET THIS GUY A SEAT?
THIS GUY NEEDS A SEAT REAL BAD..
THANK YOU

I THINK I'VE GOT HIS NUMBER HERE...
BIP BIP
YEAH... I'M STRANDED HERE IN A REAL BAD WAY SO...
IF YOU COULD GIVE ME A CALL, AH...
SO ARE YOU FROM SEATTLE?

WELL, I MOVED HERE FROM FLORIDA
I GOT IN OVER MY HEAD DOWN THERE
THEN I GOT THAT CLEARED UP AND I MOVED HERE TO GET BACK ON MY FEET
BUT THINGS DIDN'T PAN OUT REALLY..
AND NOW I DON'T...

WELL
YOU'VE GOT ONE FRIEND AND THAT'S JESUS CHRIST
THAT'S RIGHT
HE'LL NEVER LEAVE YOU TO SATAN, NEVER
NEVER

YOU'VE GOT THAT ALL FOLDED DIFFERENTLY?
YEP
SO YOU CAN TELL THE DIFFERENCE
YOU'RE SMART.

HERE. I HOPE THIS HELPS
OH, THANK YOU BROTHER
WELL, I HOPE THINGS WORK OUT FOR YOU
I'M SURE THEY WILL.

I'M HERE LEARNING TO BECOME SELF RELIANT
I'M TAKING CLASSES, SO I CAN, YOU KNOW, LEARN HOW TO COOK AND THINGS
HOW OLD ARE YOU?
I'M TWENTY ONE
YOU'RE JUST A YOUNG GUY

I USED TO BE PART OF THIS GROUP CALLED FAITH UNLIMITED...
WE'D GO TO PRISONS AND SING, MINISTER TO THE PRISONERS...
AND THAT...
THAT WAS THE LAST TIME I FELT CLOSE TO GOD...

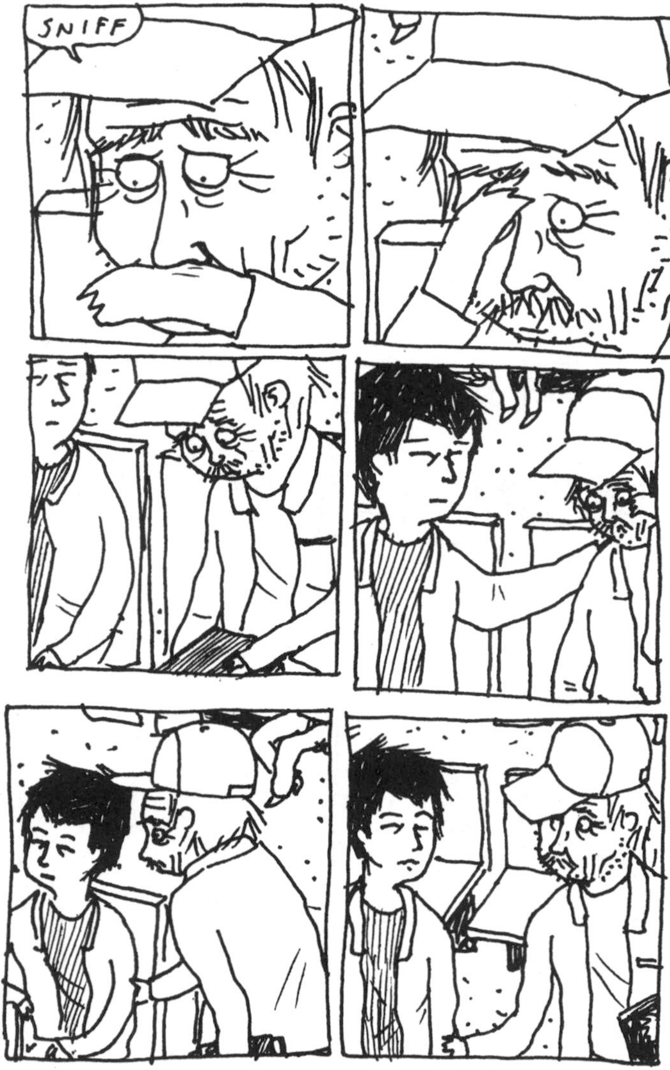
SNIFF

EXCUSE US
KLAK KLAK
KLAK KLAK
WHICH BUS IS THIS THE LINE FOR?
VANCOUVER.
THANKS
FIN

ADVENTURES IN MARY-LAND!
SEPTEMBER 6-7 2002

AFTER THE CONVENTION ENDS FOR THE DAY, WE SPEND A HALF HOUR TRYING TO FIND A RESTAURANT THAT'S STILL OPEN...
WHAT? DOES THIS TOWN SHUT DOWN AT 7:00 OR WHAT?
DO YOU HAVE THE DIRECTIONS?
YEAH.
WAIT, WASN'T THAT OUR TURN BACK THERE?
DAMMIT
I THINK WE TURN HERE... ALL THESE SIGNS ARE COVERED BY TREES...
SHOULDN'T WE HAVE COME TO 295 BY NOW?
I HAVEN'T SEEN ANY SIGNS...
UH... JEFF, ISN'T THAT THE CAPITOL? AND THE WASHINGTON MONUMENT?

UH... WE DIDN'T SEE THAT ON THE WAY...
WE MUST'VE GONE THE WRONG WAY ON 495?
HERE... JUST GET OFF AT THE NEXT EXIT...
I'LL JUST TURN AROUND HERE...
WAIT... ARE YOU SURE THIS ISN'T ONE WAY?
UH... I DIDN'T SEE ANY SIGNS...
OH SHIT!
SORRY.

WE HAVE TO DRIVE FOR MILES TO FIND A PLACE WE CAN PULL OVER...
WELL, THE GUY WOULDN'T GIVE ME DIRECTIONS, BUT I LOOKED AT A MAP..
WAIT.. 295 DOESN'T GO ANY FURTHER?
LET'S JUST CALL ERIC...
BUT IT'S SO LATE...
SOON...
UH... YEAH... WE'RE ON 495...
WHAT? THE PARKWAY IS 295? WHY DON'T THE SIGNS SAY THAT?
THE NEXT DAY WE SEE A MAP AND IT ALL MAKES SENSE...
PAUL'S SISTER'S PLACE
295 (PARKWAY)
BETHESDA
WASHINGTON DC
495 (BELTWAY)
IT'S LIKE YOU NEED TRAINING TO DRIVE AROUND HERE...
NOW I UNDERSTAND WHY POLITICS ARE SO MESSED UP...

MY CONSPIRACY TO NOT SELL TO YOU THE NEW 'GARDEN STATE' DVD
WHERE DO YOU HAVE 'GARDEN STATE'?
OH, WE DON'T YET. OUR NEW RELEASE SHIPMENT WAS DELAYED BY THE SNOW STORM. WE DON'T KNOW WHEN IT'LL GET HERE, BUT HOPEFULLY TODAY.
SO WHEN WILL IT GET HERE TODAY?
PROBABLY THIS AFTERNOON, BUT WE CAN'T SAY FOR SURE.
WELL, I CAN'T GO HOME WITHOUT IT. YOU'LL HAVE IT TODAY THOUGH?
WE SHOULD.
ARE YOU SURE YOU DON'T HAVE A COPY IN BACK?
NO, WE DO ALL OF OUR RECEIVING RIGHT HERE, AND I'VE BEEN HERE TODAY AND YESTERDAY SO I'M POSITIVE WE DON'T.

SO WHEN WILL YOU HAVE IT?
I'M NOT SURE. LATER TODAY PROBABLY, POSSIBLY NOT UNTIL TOMORROW
THIS IS GETTING REALLY ANNOYING. YOU DON'T HAVE ANY IDEA WHEN IT'LL BE HERE TODAY?
MA'AM, I REALLY HAVE NO IDEA. IF I DID, I WOULD TELL YOU.
YOU ARE SUCH A SNOT!
REALLY, I'M NOT.
YOU ARE! EVERY TIME I COME IN HERE YOU ARE SUCH A SNOT TO ME!

ACTUALLY, MA'AM, YOU'RE KIND OF A SNOT.
THAT IS SO INAPPROPRIATE I CANNOT BELIEVE YOU! I AM GOING TO TALK TO YOUR MANAGER, WHAT IS YOUR NAME?
MY NAME IS JEFF.
UH!
FIVE MINUTES LATER
DID SHE TALK TO YOU?
OH YEAH. WE KNOW HER. SHE'S ALWAYS PAYING WITH STORE CREDITS AND SHE'S REALLY RUDE..
HERE SHE COMES-
WHERE ARE YOUR HOWIE DAY CD'S?

RIGHT HERE. THIS IS HIS NEWEST.
YOU KNOW I JUST GOT OFF THE PHONE WITH MY SISTER AND SHE KNEW JUST WHO I WAS TALKING ABOUT
SHE HAD A RUN-IN WITH YOU TOO, YOU'RE THE RUDEST EMPLOYEE.
WELL, THAT'S YOUR OPINION, YOU'RE ENTITLED TO IT.
WELL WHY DON'T YOU SHOW ME WHERE YOUR O.C. SOUNDTRACKS ARE, SINCE YOU'RE MR. HELPFUL TODAY?
OVER HERE.
YOU KNOW, YOU'RE REALLY INAPPROPRIATE W-
MA'AM! REALLY, CAN WE JUST DROP THIS? IT'S RIDICULOUS.
NO, WE CAN'T DROP THIS, YOU BLAH BLAH BLAH BLA
YOU HAVE TO HELP HER. I'M DONE.

OH MY GOD, STAR WARS: EPISODE III OPENS TOMORROW!
WE'VE BEEN WAITING 25 YEARS FOR THIS!
9:00 PM
THE ORIGINAL STAR WARS FILMS ARE TAINTED BY OUR NOSTALGIA... THE LAST TWO HAVE BEEN HORRIBLE!
DO YOU WANT TO GO TO THE MIDNIGHT SHOW?
OKAY
9:30 PM
THE MIDNIGHT SHOW IS SOLD OUT... THERE'S A 3A.M. SHOW
WE'LL HAVE TO STAY UP ALL NIGHT
10:00 PM
MORE SODA!
MORE COFFEE!
12:30 AM
THIS LINE IS HUGE, DOES THE NEW TODD SOLONDZ FILM OPEN TONIGHT?
1:30 AM
HEH HEH
1:31 AM

WOOHOO!
YAYY!
HOORAY!
YIPPEE!
WHY IS EVERYONE CHEERING? THE MOVIE HASN'T EVEN STARTED.
CLAP CLAP CLAP CLAP CLAP CLAP CLAP CLAP CLAP CLAP
3:15 AM
I LOVE YOU, BECAUSE LOVE IS LOVING MY LOVE FOR YOU -- WITH LOVE!
NOW I UNDERSTAND WHY HE BECOMES DARTH VADER
5:00 AM
THAT WAS... UM...
SHIT, I HAVE TO BE TO WORK IN AN HOUR!
6:30 AM
SEVENTYFIVE YEARS AGO, THE SURREALIST FILM L'AGE D'OR OPENED TO SIMILAR, SPECTACULAR RESULTS!
WE'LL SHOW YOU THERE'S STILL CHRISTIANS IN FRANCE!
IT'S AMAZING HOW FAR FILM HAS COME!
YOU WENT TO THE 3AM SHOW? WAS IT WORTH IT?
2:00 PM

HAPPY ST. PATTY'S DAY!
THERE'S A LOT OF DRUNKS OUT...
WELL, IT IS 5 PM.
DON'T CHALLENGE ME.
DON'T EVER FUCKING CHALLENGE ME!
IF YOU TELL ME PUNCH THAT GUY IN THE FACE, I WILL.
DODGE!
KEEP WALKING, BITCH!

YUMMY COFFEE
OH, WE'VE BEEN SELLING YOUR COMICS FOR YEARS, THEY'RE REALLY GOOD
FOR 'YEARS?'
YEAH, SINCE THE LATE 80'S? 90'S MAYBE? HAVENT YOU..?
UHHHH
TOKYOPOP
YOU DID THAT COMIC 'YUMMY FUR'?
OH. ACTUALLY THAT'S CHESTER BROWN..
OH, I'M SORRY, OH GOSH...
IT'S OKAY, REALLY.
I'M--
AH!
OH MY GOSH! I'M SO SORRY!

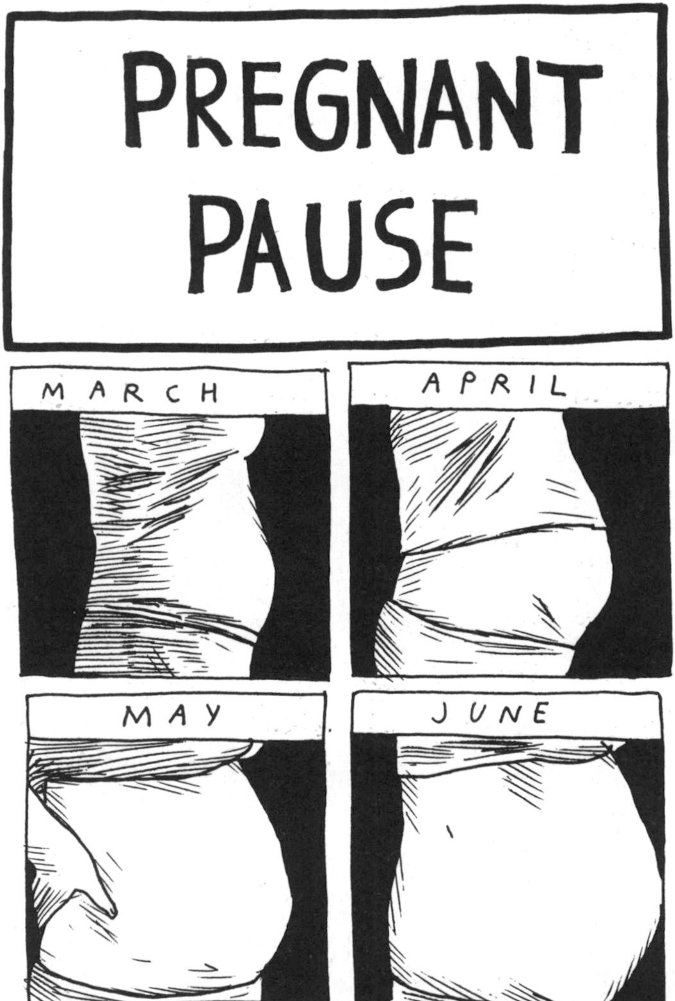
PREGNANT PAUSE
MARCH
APRIL
MAY
JUNE

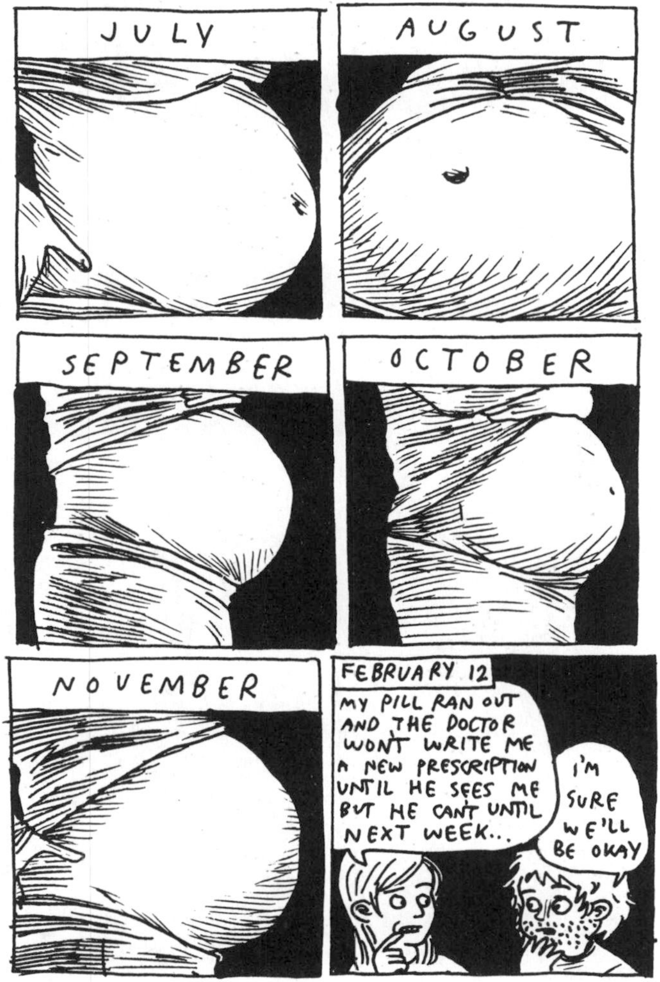
JULY
AUGUST
SEPTEMBER
OCTOBER
NOVEMBER
FEBRUARY 12
MY PILL RAN OUT AND THE DOCTOR WON'T WRITE ME A NEW PRESCRIPTION UNTIL HE SEES ME BUT HE CAN'T UNTIL NEXT WEEK...
I'M SURE WE'LL BE OKAY

MARCH 1
MUSIC, CALL ON LINE TWO
HELLO, MUSIC, THIS IS JEFF
HI, IT'S ME
I'M AT THE AIRPORT AND I SAW THESE KIDS, AND I THOUGHT, I WANT A BABY..
OH, HUH, YEAH... HA HA... HEH
I KNOW, I KNOW
SHE SOUNDED KIND OF EMOTIONAL... WHAT A STRANGE CALL...
OBLIVIOUSNESS

MARCH 2
SHE SOUNDED KIND OF UPSET ON THE PHONE. IS SOMETHING GOING ON?
SO...
I'M PREGNANT.
OH. UH. OKAY.

MARCH 10
HM, WHERE ARE THE NEW TOWELS? OH WELL
LATER
JEFF, CALL ON LINE THREE
THIS IS JEFF
WHAT'S WRONG?!
WHAT'S WRONG? DID SOMETHING HAPPEN?
SOMETHING HAPPENED?
HUH?
IS THERE SOMETHING WRONG? ARE YOU ANGRY?
WHAT? NO-WHAT DO YOU MEAN?
SOB
YOU DIDN'T USE THE NEW TOWELS!
OH. I DIDN'T KNOW WHERE YOU PUT THEM.
SOB

MARCH 12
SO, DOUG SAYS YOU HAVE NEWS?
UM, MOM, JENNIFER IS PREGNANT
THANKS, DOUG!
SO WHAT DOES THIS MEAN, JEFF?
WELL, WE'RE GOING TO HAVE A BABY
BUT WHAT DOES THIS MEAN?
WE'RE NOT GETTING MARRIED, MOM
(NOT YET, ANYWAY)
MARCH 24
I DON'T SEE...
RIGHT THERE
BUT SHE SAID THERE'S NO YOLK SAC YET?
WHAT IF SOMETHING'S WRONG? WE SHOULDN'T HAVE TOLD PEOPLE YET.
WELL, YOU STARTED BY TELLING YOUR SISTER...
YOU TOLD YOUR BROTHER
...AND YOUR MOM. EMILY. ANNEMARIE.
OKAY, OKAY!

APRIL 15
HEY JEFF, CALL FOR YOU
?
WHERE ARE YOU? WHAT HAPPENED? IS EVERYTHING OKAY?!
WHAT? I'M AT THE CONVENTION. I'M FINE...
YOU HAD ME WORRIED SICK! I THOUGHT YOU WERE DEAD! WHY DIDN'T YOU CALL LAST NIGHT?! YOU SAID YOU'D CALL!
I SAID I'D TRY TO CALL
YOU CAN'T DO THIS ANYMO
GOT A FAMILY AND IT'S
ORTANT AND I AM SO AN
MAKES ME FEEL? AND
UM
UH HUH. I'M SORRY. OKAY. YEAH. I'M SORRY
I'M DEFINITELY GETTING A CELLPHONE WHEN I GET BACK HOME.
?

APRIL 24
I'M REALLY WORRIED ABOUT THIS FIRST TRI-MESTER SCREENING
MAYBE WE SHOULD GO SHOPPING TO DISTRACT YOU.
OKAY, DO YOU THINK WE HAVE ENOUGH BOOKS?
UM, YEAH
PREGNANCY
NONE OF THESE CLOTHES FIT... AND THIS HEARTBURN IS KILLING ME...
I WANT MY BODY BACK.
...AND SO WHEN WE LOOK AT ALL THE FACTORS TOGETHER, THE ODDS ARE THAT YOU'RE PROBABLY OKAY IN ALL LIKELIHOOD.
MORE OR LESS.
DO YOU FEEL BETTER NOW?

APRIL 30
JEFF! WAKE UP!
HUH? WHAT?
I NEED BACON. NOW.
IT'S NOT EVEN SIX AM. WHERE ARE WE GOING TO GET BACON?
COULD I GET SOME MORE COFFEE?
THAT NIGHT
JEFF!
HUH?
I CAN'T SLEEP.
I'VE GOT NAUSEA.

MAY 19
HEY! YOUR HAIRCUT LOOKS GOOD.
SWEET! I TOTALLY REMEMBERED TO SAY SOMETHING RIGHT AWAY! GOOD JOB, JEFF!
NO IT'S NOT, IT LOOKS AWFUL! I JUST WANTED IT A LITTLE SHORTER, NOW IT'LL NEVER GROW BACK!
AND NOW I HAVE TO GO TO THIS OPENING AND LOOK STUPID
PAT PAT
SOB
LATER
SEE? YOU LOOK NICE...
SNIFF
MY BOOBS ARE TOO BIG...
NO, THEY AREN'T.

MAY 24
SO JEFF, ARE YOU HOPING FOR A BOY OR GIRL?
EITHER ONE...
UNCLE JEFF SAID HE WANTS A GIRL.
WHAT?
YEAH. SO THEN HE DOESN'T HAVE TO TAKE CARE OF THE BABY AS MUCH.
I TOTALLY DIDN'T SAY THAT.
MM-HM.
YES YOU DID.
MAY 25
LET'S SEE... NO, THIS WAS A BAD ROOMMATE I HAD, THIS WAS A KID I DIDN'T LIKE IN HIGH SCHOOL. THIS IS MY NEPHEW'S NAME, THIS IS MY COUSIN'S KID...
WOULDN'T GO WITH THE LAST NAME BROWN, WOULD HAVE THE SAME INITIALS AS YOU, EX-BOYFRIEND, THIS ONE I JUST DON'T LIKE...
UM, WHAT NAMES ARE LEFT NOW?
UM...

MAY 28
SHOULD WE GET THE BABY BAPTISED?
BUT WE'RE NOT CHRISTIAN.
OUR FAMILIES MIGHT LIKE IT IF WE DID... YOUR DAD COULD DO THE BAPTISM.
SO
MY DAD SAYS HE COULD DO IT, BUT WE'D HAVE TO BE MEMBERS OF A CHURCH.
I GUESS THE BABY CAN DECIDE LATER...
JUNE 4
HEY! WHAT TOOK YOU SO LONG?
I GOT WAYLAID BY SOME WOMAN WHO INSISTED ON GIVING ME A BUNCH OF ADVICE ABOUT GETTING THE BABY TO SLEEP.

JUNE 11
WHOOOAAA!
HEY!
WHAT?
OKAY, FIRST YOU AND YOUR BODY PILLOW TAKE UP MORE THAN HALF THE BED...
BUT I LOVE MY BODY PILLOW.
...AND THEN YOU KEEP STEALING THE COVERS!
I'M SORRY.
COME BACK TO BED, HONEY...

JUNE 16
... AND... LET'S SEE... C'MON, MOVE YOUR FOOT... THAT'S A REALLY ACTIVE BABY!
I MAY HAVE MADE SOME COFFEE...
THERE! IT'S A BOY.
CONGRATULATIONS!
ARE YOU DISAPPOINTED?
NO, ARE YOU?
NO.
SO SHOULD WE GET HIM CIRCUMCISED?
I DON'T THINK WE SHOULD.
BUT DO YOU THINK HE'LL FEEL WEIRD IF HE LOOKS... DIFFERENT?
I DON'T THINK THERE SHOULD BE ANY CUTTING UNLESS IT'S ABSOLUTELY NECESSARY.

JULY 17
HE KICKED! I FELT IT!
HAPPY BIRTHDAY!
I THINK HE'S TRYING TO COMMUNICATE... DO YOU WANT TO BE A HOCKEY PLAYER?
HM. NOTHING... DO YOU WANT TO BE AN ULTIMATE FIGHTER?
UH...DO YOU WANT TO BE A MINISTER?
KICK!
KICK!
KICK!
KICK!
KICK!
KICK!
KICK!
KICK!

JULY 31
POP
OH NO! THE POWER WENT OUT AGAIN?!
I HOPE IT'S NOT OFF FOR THREE HOURS LIKE LAST NIGHT...
8 PM
MY APARTMENT DOESN'T HAVE THE AIR CONDITIONERS OR FANS...
SAME WITH THE NEW APARTMENT.
9 PM
THE COFFEE SHOPS WILL ALL BE CLOSED THIS LATE AT NIGHT.
10PM
COM ED SAYS THE ESTIMATE TO HAVE POWER AGAIN IS TWO O'CLOCK...
IN THE MORNING?
NO, TOMORROW AFTERNOON
11 PM
JEFF, I CAN'T TAKE THIS ANYMORE...
WHAT CAN WE DO?
12AM
I CAN'T BELIEVE WE'RE PAYING RENT ON THREE APARTMENTS AND PAYING TO SPEND THE NIGHT IN A HOTÆL.

AUGUST 8
I LOVE YOU, I LOVE YOU, I LOVE YOU.
YOU JUST TOLD THAT DIET COKE "I LOVE YOU" MORE THAN YOU TELL ME.
AUGUST 14
JEFFFF!
WHAT?
DID YOU DRINK THE LAST DIET COKE?!!
UM...
NO?

AUGUST 17
DO YOU THINK THIS IS A BAD SIGN FOR US MOVING IN TOGETHER?
WHAT? NO, WHY?
THOSE WERE THE WORST MOVERS EVER! THEY WERE TWO HOURS LATE AND THE FIRST THING THEY DID WAS TAKE A MASSIVE DUMP IN THE BATHROOM!
THEY DAMAGED A BUNCH OF OUR FURNITURE, MARKED UP THE WHOLE STAIRWELL, AND YOU HAD TO DISASSEMBLE THE BED FOR THEM..
AND THEN THEY TRIED TO CHARGE US FOR WORKING AN EXTRA HOUR BECAUSE THEY WORKED UNTIL TEN AFTER!
LOOK, THEY EVEN LEFT THEIR PEN AND IT LEAKED ALL OVER THIS BOOKSHELF.
WE'LL LAUGH ABOUT THIS LATER.
MUCH LATER.

SEPTEMBER 2
DID YOU FINISH IT YET?
NAOMI WOLF "MISCONCEPTIONS"
YEAH... IT'S KIND OF SCARY.
I KNOW. DO YOU THINK WE'RE DOING THE RIGHT THING? DO WE LIKE MY DOCTOR?
YEAH. I MEAN, I DON'T KNOW. MAYBE?
MAYBE WE SHOULD BE USING A MIDWIFE.
SEPTEMBER 3
I'M SO TIRED THIS MORNING...
WHY?
BECAUSE I WAS UP SO LATE... DON'T YOU REMEMBER MAKING ME CRY?
I REMEMBER YOU CRYING, BUT I DON'T REMEMBER THE "MAKING YOU" PART.
!

SEPTEMBER 21
EEEEEEEEEEPP
EEEEEEEEPP
EEEEEEEPPP
WILL YOU STOP?!!
HUH? WHAT?
YOU'RE OUT HERE MAKING THAT AWFUL NOISE, AND I'M IN THERE THROWING UP!
OH.
I COULDN'T HEAR YOU THROWING UP OVER MY TAPE GUN.
SORRY.
ALL TAPED UP NOW.

OCTOBER 7
WE ARE SO LATE... WE CAN BARELY TAKE CARE OF A CAT, HOW CAN WE TAKE CARE OF A BABY? AND DO YOU REMEMBER THE PIZZA FIRE?
YOU'RE HERE FOR THE BABY CPR CLASS?
YEAH
EXCUSE US
SORRY
OOP!
BUMP!
OPE! OOH...
CRASH!

OCTOBER 21
MAYBE THE MIDWIFE HAS A LIST OF PEDIATRICIANS?
WELL, I FOUND THIS ONE. OH WAIT... "USING THE PRINCIPLES OF MEDICINE, AS DIRECTED BY GOD..."
I WANT OUR PEDIATRICIAN TO BE DIRECTED BY SCIENCE.
OCTOBER 23
ARE WE GOING TO SAVE THE CORD BLOOD?
I DON'T KNOW... I DON'T THINK SO. IT'S EXPENSIVE, BUT IS IT EVEN HELPFUL?
AND MORE IMPORTANTLY, CAN I EAT THE PLACENTA?
NO.

OCTOBER 28
HI
HI
CAN YOU TAKE MY SHOES OFF?
YEAH.
I'M JUST SO TIRED AND SORE AND EMOTIONAL.
YEAH.
HOW WAS YOUR LAST DAY OF WORK?
OKAY. I'M SO GLAD TO BE ON MATERNITY LEAVE.
SO WHO'D YOU CRY IN FRONT OF TODAY?

NOVEMBER 2
WELL, I KNOW YOUR DUE DATE IS TOMORROW, BUT...
IT DOESN'T LOOK LIKE HE'S READY TO COME OUT. WE'LL HAVE YOU COME BACK AND HOOK UP THE FETAL MONITOR TO MAKE SURE EVERYTHING'S OKAY.
I'M SO TIRED OF BEING PREGNANT...
SO UNTIL SOMETHING HAPPENS, JUST RELAX, AND ENJOY THIS TIME AS A COUPLE.
I'M SURE IT'LL HAPPEN SOON...
"ENJOY THIS TIME AS A COUPLE?" THAT'S WHAT GOT US INTO THIS IN THE FIRST PLACE!

NOVEMBER 7
HI, WE'RE HERE FOR AN ULTRA SOUND... "A WOMAN'S PLACE" SET UP THE APPOINTMENT?
RIGHT, COME WITH ME
OKAY. HM. ALRIGHT.
WELL, THE BABY LOOKS FINE, HE LOOKS LIKE A BIG, HEALTHY BABY...
I'D SAY HE'LL BE ABOUT EIGHT AND A HALF POUNDS, AND I'D ESTIMATE THE DUE DATE SHOULD ACTUALLY BE THE 16th
ANOTHER WEEK?! THAT'S NOT WHAT I WANT TO HEAR!
BUT HE'S HEALTHY, THAT'S GOOD.

NOVEMBER 16
HOW WAS THE ACCUPUNCTURE?
GOOD. I DONT FEEL LIKE ANYTHING IS HAPPENING THOUGH.
WELL, WE'LL GET TO THE HOSPITAL, AND THEN IT'S ONLY A MATTER OF TIME, RIGHT?
8:10 PM
YOU'RE NOT REALLY DILATED AT ALL...
THIS CREAM WILL GET THINGS STARTED. WE'LL LET IT WORK OVER NIGHT...
I'LL BE BACK TOMORROW MORNING AND HOPEFULLY THINGS WILL BE MOVING ALONG...

12:45 AM
OH, I THINK MY WATER BROKE...
HERE, WE'LL GET YOU IN THE SHOWER...
OH...
AANNHHH
JEFFF?
OH MY GOD, THAT HURTS...
THAT ONE WAS A MINUTE LONG
ANNNHHH
I THOUGHT CONTRACTIONS WERE SUPPOSED TO START SLOWLY?! THIS ISN'T WHAT I SIGNED UP FOR!

3:00 AM
OH MY GOD, I'M GOING TO DIE!
AAANNHHH
* AT THE TIME, MODESTY WAS GONE AND JENNIFER WAS NAKED... HOWEVER, MODESTY HAS SINCE RETURNED. -ED.
DID YOU CALL ABI?!
YEAH, SHE SHOULD BE HERE SOON
AAAAANNHHHHH
OH GOOD, SHE'S HERE
IT'S OKAY, HERE, LET'S SIT YOU LIKE THIS...
THAT'S WHAT I TRIED TO SAY
SHUT UP AANNHHH

9:00 AM
IT LOOKS LIKE YOU'RE DILATED TO EIGHT CM...
IT SHOULDN'T BE LONG
ENNHHMH
OH WAIT... IT'S ACTUALLY MORE LIKE FOUR CM...
9:30 AM
IS IT BAD IF I GET THE EPIDURAL?
NO, IT'S NOT... YOU COULD USE SOME SLEEP...
11:30 AM
AAGGHHH! CAN WE GET THIS EPIDURAL TOPPED OFF?

4:30 PM
AGGHHH! GO AWAY!
ME?
NO, THE PAIN.
AGGHHH! SHUT UP!
ME?
5:10 PM
AGGHHH! TAKE HIM OUT!
OKAY, I THINK IT'S TIME TO PUSH...
URG
YOU MIGHT WANT TO PUT YOUR SHOES ON, JEFF

7:00 PM
AAAGHHH! I FEEL LIKE I'M GOING TO TAKE A SHIT!
THAT'S OKAY, SWEETIE, MAKE POO POO.
HUFF HUFF
PAT PAT
MAKE POO POO
AAAGHH!
7:05 PM
WHAT THE FUCK? IS SOMETHING WRONG? SHE'S TRYING TO PUT THE BABY BACK IN?!
AAHH! HIS HEAD IS SMOOSHED?!
AAAHH
IT LOOKED LIKE THIS:
BUT IT WAS ACTUALLY JUST THE TOP OF HIS HEAD, AND THE MIDWIFE WAS STOPPING HIM FROM COMING OUT TOO FAST, TO PREVENT TEARING

7:10 PM
ANGGHHH
THERE, YOU DID IT, YOU DID IT
OH MY GOD
IS HE OKAY?
WANHHH
HE'S GOT A CONE-HEAD... AND HE LOOKS BLUE...
OKAY, NOW WHAT?

TO PHOENIX
I'M SORRY I MISSED YOU

ON SATURDAY NIGHT MY BROTHER, SOME FRIENDS AND I WENT TO SEE THE IFL*
WHAT PERCENTAGE OF THE PEOPLE HERE DO YOU THINK ARE WEARING BLACK HOODED SWEATSHIRTS?
I'D SAY 85%
* INTERNATIONAL FIGHT LEAGUE
I GOT HOME AFTER MIDNIGHT
THANKS FOR THE RIDE
UH-OH
WHAT ARE THEY DOING STILL UP?
THIS ISN'T A GOOD SIGN...

HERE.
WHAT'S GOING ON?
WENHH
HE'S SICK, HE'S BEEN THROWING UP ALL NIGHT.
OH NO!
MEH
WHY ARE YOU GIVING HIM TO ME?
ENHHH
WHAT DO YOU MEAN? HE HASN'T SLEPT AT ALL. I NEED A BREAK.
YEAH, BUT HE'S ALREADY THROWN UP ON YOU.
MEHN

ON MONDAY, FRIENDS FROM NEW YORK WERE IN TOWN...
I DON'T THINK WE CAN MEET UP--- OSCAR'S REALLY SICK. NO, HOPEFULLY WE DON'T GET IT... HA HA!
IRONIC LAUGHTER
HE'S STILL NOT EATING...
POOR GUY..
PICK
PICK
I HOPE HE SLEEPS BETTER TONIGHT.
ME TOO
AND HE DID SLEEP BETTER THAT NIGHT..

HOWEVER, I SPENT MOST OF THE NIGHT ON THE KITCHEN FLOOR AND IN THE BATHROOM...
OH CRAP!
GURGLE
GURGLE
GURGLE
URMPHH
NOTE CONVENIENT PLACEMENT OF SINK IN RELATION TO TOILET
OOOOOOOHHHHH
WHERE'S MY SYMPATHY?

TUESDAY
WHY DON'T YOU GO BACK TO BED?
I CAN'T SLEEP
IN THERE A LOT
DO YOU WANT SOME LEFTOVER STEW? COFFEE? BANANA? SANDWHICH?
NO, NO, NO, NO..
HERE'S SOME SALTINES AND GINGERALE
THANKS
MUNCH MUNCH MUNCH

ARE YOU GOING TO GO TO PHOENIX TOMORROW?
I DON'T KNOW.. MY HEAD HURTS...
I CAN'T IMAGINE FLYING RIGHT NOW...
MAYBE I'LL SEE IF I FEEL BETTER IN THE MORNING.
HOWEVER...
UH OH
URMPPHHGGHH

OHHHHHHHHH...
MAYBE I SHOULDN'T GO... I SHOULD EMAIL THEM IF I DON'T...
BLEARGGG
GO AND BE SICK BUT SOLDIER THROUGH IT...
...OR STAY AND FEEL GUILTY ABOUT NOT MAKING THE SIGNING..
OHHHHHH..
GUILT IT IS.
SORRY, SAMURAI COMICS...
FIN

FINE PRINT
OR
SOME THOUGHTS ON PERSONAL EXPERIENCES DEALING WITH HEALTH CARE IN AMERICA
OCTOBER 2008
OSCAR! WHAT IS THAT? DON'T PUT THAT IN YOUR MOUTH!
C'MERE! HM, IT'S GONE NOW... WHAT'D YOU EAT? BLUE CHALK? CANDY?
LATER
HE SEEMS LIKE HE DOESN'T FEEL GOOD OR SOMETHING..
AS OUR TWO YEAR OLD FREAKED OUT MORE AND MORE, WE PUT TOGETHER WHAT MUST HAVE HAPPENED
NO!
NO NAP!
WAAUGHH!
EVEN BY TODDLER STANDARDS, OSCAR'S BEHAVIOR WAS ODD
NO FISHIES! BLUEBERRIES!
NOOO!
WANT FISHIES!
NO BLUEBERRY! WANT CORN!

RELATIVE BABYSITTING
PURSE UNDER STROLLER
PRESCRIPTION A.D.D. MEDICINE
AND SO, AT THE E.R.
WELL, THE GOOD NEWS IS THAT THE EFFECTS OF THE PILL WILL BE TEMPORARY AND HE'S GOING TO BE FINE.
NOOOOOOO!
WITH THE LIFE OF THE PILL, HE'S PEAKING NOW. BASICALLY, IT'S LIKE BEING ON SPEED FOR HIM.
NOOO
ONE NURSE TRIED TO GIVE HIM A MOUSE FOR COMFORT...
NOOOO! OUT THERE! NOOO!
HE WAS ALSO AGITATED BY VARIOUS LIGHTS..
NOOO!
WE'LL GIVE HIM A SMALL DOSE OF SEDATIVE, AND YOU'LL BE ABLE TO GO HOME IN TWENTY MINUTES.
NOOOO!

TWENTY MINUTES LATER
THE PILL STILL NEEDS TO WORK THROUGH HIS SYSTEM, BUT YOU CAN GO HOME NOW.
BLARGGGHH!
HERE'S YOUR PAPERS, AND IT'S A SEVENTY-FIVE DOLLAR CO-PAY
BACK HOME, HE STARTED TO GET HIS APPETITE BACK.
HE'S ACTING GOOFY NOW...
FINALLY, HE FELL ASLEEP.
A COUPLE WEEKS LATER WAS THE RUDE AWAKENING...
IT'S THE BILL FOR THE E.R. VISIT... $587.00

AND
IT'S A BILL FOR THE E.R. DOCTOR. $260.00
BUT I THOUGHT WE PAID...
WE SHOULD'VE KNOWN HAVING INSURANCE DOESN'T MEAN YOU'RE COVERED...
AS LONG AS YOU HAVE HIM HERE, DO YOU WANT HIS NEXT VACCINATION?
WE TOOK HIM IN TO MAKE SURE HE DIDN'T HAVE AN EAR INFECTION, A WEEK BEFORE HIS SCHEDULED CHECK-UP
WAIT, WHAT DO YOU MEAN VACCINES AREN'T COVERED YET?
IF WE HAD WAITED TO GET THOSE SHOTS, WE WOULD HAVE SAVED $2,500.00
OF COURSE, IT SAYS RIGHT HERE IN OUR INFORMATION PACKET.
ACTUALLY, OUR PROBLEMS WITH INSURANCE AND OSCAR STARTED BEFORE HE WAS BORN...
AS LONG AS IT'S AT A HOSPITAL, YES, A MIDWIFE BIRTH IS COVERED.
OKAY, GOOD
...OR RATHER, SOON AFTER HE WAS BORN.
I'M SORRY, BUT IT'S NOT ENOUGH TO HAVE A DOCTOR ON CALL, THERE HAS TO BE A DOCTOR IN THE ROOM FOR THE BIRTH.
BUT--

EVEN BACK IN HIGH SCHOOL WHEN I WAS DIAGNOSED WITH CROHN'S DISEASE, NO ONE TOLD ME WHAT IT WOULD MEAN LATER
IF YOU HAVE CROHN'S, I'M AFRAID WE CAN'T SELL YOU A POLICY.
EVEN THOUGH I HAVEN'T HAD CROHN'S RELATED HEALTH ISSUES IN 15 YEARS SINCE THE DIAGNOSIS
WITH YOUR CASE HISTORY, I THINK THEY MISDIAGNOSED YOU WITH CROHN'S...
CAN YOU WRITE A LETTER SAYING THAT?
NO.
STILL, WE HOPE THAT THINGS WILL CHANGE BEFORE OSCAR HAS TO WORRY ABOUT THEM THE WAY WE DO
EARLY VOTIN
BEEP BEEP
HOLD STILL, OSCAR
BEEP BEEP BEEP
OH NO, DON'T!
OSCAR, NO!
IF HE PUSHED THAT BUTTON, IT WOULD'VE ERASED ALL THE VOTES FOR THE DAY
WE'RE DOING WHAT WE CAN TO MAKE THINGS BETTER...

WHY NOT AUTOBIOGRAPHY?
WITH MY AUTOBIOGRAPHICAL COMICS, I TRY TO STAY AS TRUE TO MY MEMORIES AS I CAN, EVEN THOUGH I USUALLY HAVE TO LEAVE A LOT OF THINGS OUT. AND MEMORY TENDS TO DISTORT ANYWAY.
THERE'S A THEORY THAT YOU CAN REACH DEEPER TRUTHS SOMETIMES BY NOT ALWAYS TELLING THE TRUTH...
SO SOMETIMES I'VE FOUND IT USEFUL TO USE MY COMIC BOOK "SELF" FOR OTHER PURPOSES.
IN THE STORY "BE A MAN" I MADE FUN OF MYSELF WHILE ALSO QUESTIONING SOME OF THE CRITICISMS MY AUTOBIOGRAPHICAL WORK HAD RECEIVED.
NOT THAT THOSE CRITICISMS AREN'T VALID... AND NOT THAT THERE AREN'T SOME "TRUE" THINGS IN "BE A MAN."
ANYWAY, IT'S A FINE LINE BETWEEN MEMOIR AND FICTION, BUT FUN TO WALK ONCE IN A WHILE.

COFFEE 7-7

YOU KNOW
I THINK IF I SMOKED, MY PAUSES WOULD BECOME MORE MEANINGFUL
TAP TAP
DEFINITELY

TEST YOUR MIGHT

BITCH GET OFF THE PHONE

CRACK-THUD

the end

JEFFREY BROWN MUST DIE
THIS COMIC IS FOR SISSIES!
UGH! IT'S DRIPPING WITH SELF PITY!
AND THE 'ART' IS STRICTLY AMATEUR!
NO WONDER HE HAD TO SELF PUBLISH THIS!
HA! I CAN SEE WHY SHE DUMPED HIS SORRY ASS!
PFT! I'LL BET HE'S ACTUALLY PROUD OF THIS CRAP!
SHIT! I CAN BARELY READ THIS --- AND NOT JUST BECAUSE OF THE HORRIBLE LETTERING!
THIS BOOK IS HARDLY 'NOVEL'!
UNBEKNOWNST...
HE'S--HE'S TALKING ABOUT ME!
I'LL SHOW THEM! I'LL SHOW THEM ALL!
SKRITCH SKRITCH SKRITCH
WHO AM I KIDDING? I CAN'T WRITE ANYTHING BUT SELF ABSORBED TRIPE! I'LL NEVER WRITE ANY MEANINGFUL FICTION! I'LL NEVER DRAW ANYTHING 'COOL'!
SOB! IF ONLY SOMEONE LOVED ME!
SUDDENLY...
I'M HERE TO STOP YOUR CRYING, YOU BIG BABY!
KRAK!
the end

ACTION TELEVISION SHOW!
METAL PIPE GANG!
WE DON'T NEED THESE GUNS! EXCEPT MAYBE, LIKE, OUR MAIN GUY!
YEAH! WE'LL JUST USE MARTIAL ARTS INSTEAD!
YEAH! BUT ISN'T MARTIAL ARTS REALLY ONLY SUPPOSED TO BE USED FOR DEFENSE?
YEAH! BUT WE AREN'T EVEN GOING TO REALLY LEARN IT. AFTER ALL, WE'VE GOT ALL THESE GREAT METAL PIPES!
AAAH!
HOLY SHIT!
OOF!
KRAK!
WOW! DID YOU SEE HER BREASTS? THEY WERE AMAZING!
WHERE'D ALL THESE EMPTY BARRELS COME FROM? WE DON'T EVEN NEED THESE..!

WILLIAM, I NEED YOU
WILLIAM!
WHO SAID THIS?
BILLY!

GOD? IS THAT YOU?
BILLY!
IT'S ME, GOD!
I NEED YOU TO DO SOMETHING FOR ME, BILLY!
GO NOW!
THE ANIMALS HAVE BEEN MAKING FUN OF ME, BILLY, SO I NEED YOU TO MAKE FUN OF THEM!
GOD?
UM, OKAY... OKAY, GOD..
I'LL GO, UM, DO THAT NOW..
OOF!
WUMP

STUPID ANIMALS!
YOU CAN'T MESS WITH GOD! YOU'RE, UH, STUPID!
YOU ARE THE LEAST OF GOD'S CREATURES! YOU ARE AN INSULT TO HIS MAGNIFICENCE!
I HAVE NEVER SEEN ANIMALS AS STUPID AS YOU!
YOU AND YOUR STUPID FURRY HEADS!
STUPID, STUPID,
AIEEEE!
ACK' AIEEE!
ARGLLHR
AHIEEEE!

Construction

BIRD

Bird at the Highway

BE A MAN
I HAVE CONQUERED YOU, WOMAN!

CAMPER

JEFF-- I CAN'T... I'M SORRY
THAT'S OKAY, BABY
I CAN'T...
SHHHHH
YOU CAN DO IT, I KNOW YOU CAN

IT FEELS LIKE A DREAM
IT'S BEEN SO LONG...
SO HOW MANY TIMES HAVE YOU DONE THIS?
LET'S JUST SAY YOU'RE PART OF THE FOUR-DIGIT TERRITORY.

FIRST TIMES

DON'T WORRY, I'M CLEAN
I'LL BE GENTLE
WE DONT HAVE TO DO THIS IF YOU DON'T WANT TO... BUT I'M READY IF YOU ARE...
I KNOW WE HAVEN'T KNOWN EACH OTHER FOR LONG, BUT YOU'RE VERY SPECIAL TO ME..
HERE, YOU CAN WIPE YOURSELF OFF WITH THIS SOCK

SHE'S STRONG

SEE? I'M GOING TO HOLD YOU HERE FOREVER AND THERE'S NO WAY YOU CAN ESCAPE.
BUT..
I'M TOO STRONG
RAR
SPIN SPIN SPIN
RAR
RARRR

FRIDAY

...LEAVE A MESSAGE =BEEP=
THERESA, THIS IS JEFF, YOU SAID YOU'D BE HOME... GIVE ME A CALL..
MAN, SCREW THIS
RINGGGGG
HELLO?
HI. IT'S ME--
WELL YOU'RE TOO LATE NOW
DON'T YOU HAVE A GIRLFRIEND?
DONT WORRY, SHE LIVES IN FLORIDA

ONE LAST QUICK TIME

STAY UP FOREVER

DO YOU LOVE ME?

SLEEP

HI.
HI.
GOOD NIGHT.
I'LL SEE YOU TOMORROW MORNING.
I'M SORRY... I SLEPT ALL DAY... I RUINED YOUR WHOLE FIRST DAY HERE...
OH, THAT'S FINE. I NEEDED SOME TIME TO MYSELF AFTER THE FIFTEEN MINUTES I SPENT WITH YOU LAST NIGHT.

FAT

I'M FAT.
WELL, THEN WHY DON'T YOU GET OFF YOUR ASS AND LOSE SOME WEIGHT?
OR JUST BE COMFORTABLE WITH YOUR BODY, LIKE I AM
THAT CHICK IS HOT

JET GIRL

IF YOU COULD SLEEP WITH ANYONE IN THE WORLD WHO WOULD IT BE?
UH, THAT ONE FRIEND OF YOURS... THE BLONDE... WHAT'S HER NAME?
IF YOU COULD SLEEP WITH ANYONE, WHO WOULD IT BE?
JET GIRL.
REALLY?
DOES SHE LIVE HERE IN FLORIDA?
WE COULD CALL HER UP FOR A LITTLE THREESOME ACTION...

MY LITTLE BOOK

WAITING FOR HER TO CALL

SPRINGER

ARE YOU READY TO GO TO SEE JERRY SPRINGER?
YAY!
UH-OH
WHAT?
I THINK IM STARTING BLEEDING
OH GREAT.
HURRY UP, WE'RE GONNA BE LATE.
THERE WASNT A BATHROOM.
EW, WHAT, YOU'RE PUTTING IT IN HERE?!
EWW, GROSS!

ROACHES

UGH, I'M SO TIRED.
LET'S TAKE A "NAP" TOGETHER
WHAT?
AIEEEE!
ROACHES!
DON'T WORRY, I'LL GET THEM!
THAT'S THE LAST OF THEM!
MY HERO!
RAR!

NO KITTIES

DRAW ME SOME KITTIES NOW
OKAY
IF I DRAW ENOUGH PUSSIES, THEN I'LL BE SURE TO GET SOME PUSSY
OH, THEY'RE SO CUTE
SO ARE YOU

COOKIES

HA HA HA HA
THIS SHOW SUCKS, BUT MAYBE IF I LAUGH, WE'LL FUCK LATER
HA HA HA
DO YOU THINK THE COOKIES ARE READY?
WHAT ABOUT THESE COOKIES?

FARSCAPE

JEFF, I CAN'T TALK ANYMORE TONIGHT, I WANT TO WATCH FARSCAPE...
OH, SORRY, I DON'T WANT TO DISTRACT YOU FROM YOUR PRECIOUS NERD TELEVISION
HELLO?
FUCK YOU

PRIZE

IF YOU LOVED ME, YOU WOULD WIN THAT PINK THING FOR ME
I DON'T KNOW IF I CAN...
CRASH!

A NIGHT

NO
YOU CANT HOLD ME, OR ELSE I WONT SLEEP.
HI JEFF, I'M A SUPER MODEL LET'S GO "FOR A WALK"

ALEVE

I'VE GOT A BAD HEADACHE.
WE DON'T HAVE ANY ASPIRIN.
I COULD GO ASK AT THE FRONT DESK...
YEAH.
I'LL GET YOU MEDICINE FROM SOMEWHERE.
I'VE GOT YOUR MEDICINE HERE, BABY

TOENAILS

CAN I PAINT YOUR TOENAILS?
NO
IF WE HAVE SEX FIRST, THEN I'LL LET YOU PAINT THEM
OKAY.
UH UH
OKAY, NOW CAN I PAINT YOUR TOENAILS?
I DON'T THINK SO.

LAUNDRY

YOU ARE THE MOST AMAZING PERSON AT SEX EVER! THANK YOU SO MUCH
WHAT'RE YOU DOING? I THOUGHT WE WERE GOING TO BEST BUY.
I'M WATCHING XENA.
WHERE ARE YOUR KEYS?
I NEED TO BUY CD'S

MORNING STORY

CIGARETTE

DO YOU MIND IF I HAVE A CIGARETTE?
WELL, GIVE ME MY SHIRT BACK SO IT DOESN'T SMELL ALL NASTY
KOFF!
I BROUGHT BEER
ARE YOU GOING TO DRINK TOO?
MAYBE
HM, I'D TELL HER NOT TO DRINK BECAUSE OF HER STOMACH PROBLEMS...
... BUT SHE'LL BE EASIER THIS WAY

WEDDING

YOUR HAIR LOOKS GOOD-
I'VE GOT TO HELP. GO FIND SOMETHING TO DO.
HELLO.
HI.
SO, ARE YOU FRIENDS WITH THE BRIDE OR THE GROOM?
HOW'D YOU LIKE TO BE MY FRIEND?

SLOW DANCE

BATH

DO YOU WANT TO TAKE A SHOWER?
UM, I WAS WONDERING IF MAYBE I COULD TAKE A BATH BY MYSELF...
FINE.
OW
GURGLE
RUMBLE
SNORZZZZ

I DON'T KNOW

I'M NOT SURE WHAT TO DO.
WELL YOU KNEW IT'D BE HARD TO HAVE A LONG DISTANCE RELATIONSHIP.
BUT MAYBE WE'RE JUST TOO DIFFERENT...
I DON'T KNOW...
HUNH
WELL, WHY DON'T YOU CALL ME WHEN YOU FIGURE IT OUT
SHEESH, GIRLS ARE SILLY

THE END

SO WHY DOES YOUR MOM KEEP CALLING ME 'JOHN' NOW? HAVE YOU BEEN TALKING TO YOUR EX?
YES.
FUCK YOU. I DON'T NEED YOU.
WOO-HOO, I'M FREE!

★ COMING SOON ★

CLUMSY 2020

COMPLETELY RE-DRAWN, RE-WRITTEN AND IMPROVED! THROUGH NEW AND SOPHISTICATED TECHNIQUES, THE OLD LAME CLUMSY WILL BE RE-IMAGINED INTO A SPECTACULAR WORK OF ART!

REFURBISHING PROCESS

- ALL BEHAVIOR WILL BE CORRECTED
- MORE OUTFITS AND CHARACTERS
- DIFFERENT SIZES AND SHAPES OF PANELS --- ALL DRAWN WITH A RULER
- STORIES TO APPEAR IN CHRONOLOGICAL ORDER
- PITY FELT BY THE READER WILL BE REPLACED WITH RESPECT, ADMIRATION AND SYMPATHY
- LEGIBLE
- CRAPPY ART REPLACED BY PHOTOREALISTIC IMAGERY AND COMPUTER GENERATED EFFECTS
- SHORT SLICE OF LIFE STORIES REPLACED BY LONG, DIALOGUE FILLED CHAPTERS FULL OF INCREDIBLE DRAMA AND LIFE ALTERING EVENTS
- PICTURE ON COVER

YOU DIDN'T HAVE TO BE SUCH A FUCKER

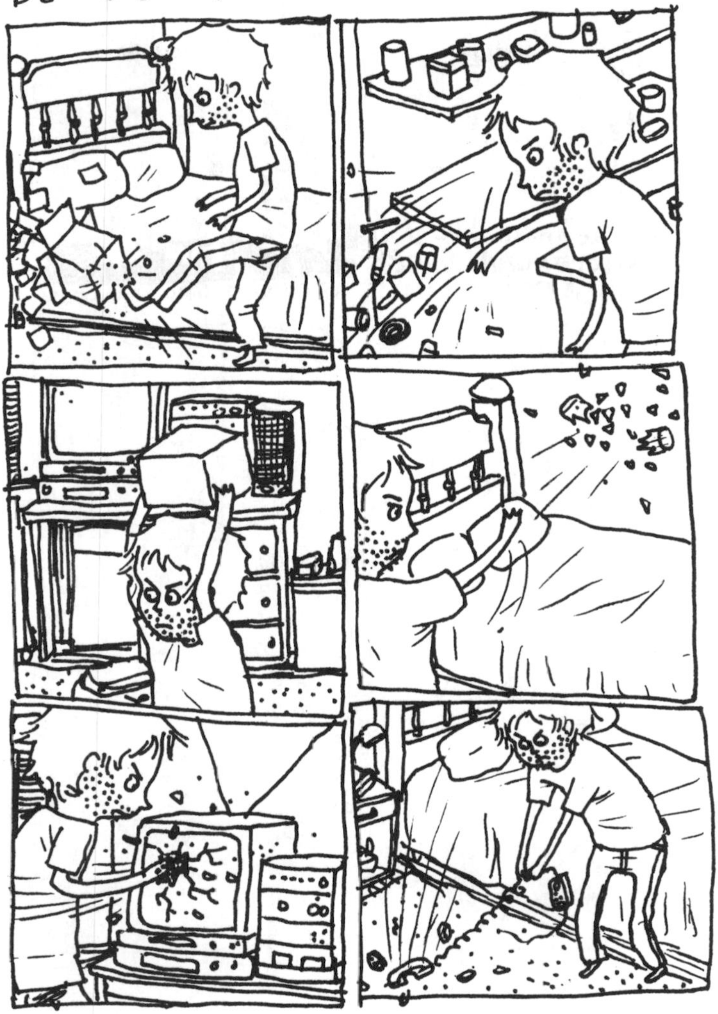

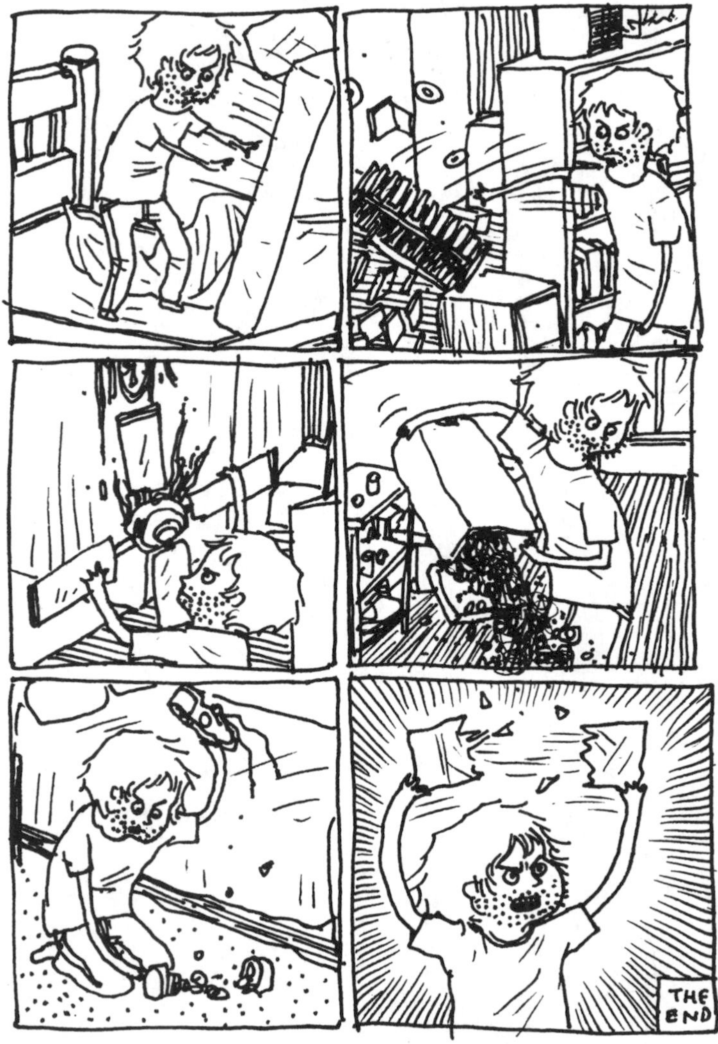
THE END

JEFFREY BROWN LIVES IN CHICAGO WITH HIS WIFE AND SON.
FIND OUT MORE AT:
WWW.JEFFREYBROWNCOMICS.COM
WRITE TO JEFFREY AT: JEFFREYBROWNRQ@HOTMAIL.COM
OR: P.O.BOX 120 DEERFIELD IL 60015-0120 USA

THANK YOU

TO ALL OF MY FRIENDS AND FAMILY ESPECIALLY JENNIFER AND OSCAR. THANKS TO EVERYONE WHO'S READ MY WORK, AND ALSO THANKS TO EVERYONE WHO'S SUPPORTED MY WORK BY PUBLISHING IT OVER THE YEARS, INCLUDING ALARM MAGAZINE, FANTAGRAPHICS, McSWEENEY'S, METRO, NEW CITY, CHICAGO READER, DRAWN & QUARTERLY FILTER MAGAZINE, AND OF COURSE TOP SHELF - SPECIAL THANKS TO CHRIS STAROS AND BRETT WARNOCK FOR THEIR SUPPORT AND KEEPING ALL OF THIS WORK IN PRINT.

ALSO AVAILABLE BY JEFFREY BROWN

CATS ARE WEIRD
INCREDIBLE CHANGE-BOTS II
SULK VOL. 4 ABOVE THE TOP
SULK VOL. 3 THE KIND OF STRENGTH THAT COMES FROM MADNESS
FUNNY MISSHAPEN BODY
SULK VOL. 2 DEADLY AWESOME
SULK VOL. 1 BIGHEAD & FRIENDS
LITTLE THINGS
INCREDIBLE CHANGE-BOTS
CAT GETTING OUT OF A BAG
I AM GOING TO BE SMALL
AEIOU: ANY EASY INTIMACY
BIGHEAD
UNLIKELY
CLUMSY